W9-CDS-278

An MD Examines

"We assume medical doctors' main expertise is figuring out body problems; however, Brad Burke defies assumptions that their knowledge ends there. His responses to age-old questions are simply too good to put down. His creative ideas and energy quickly engage me. Then, he walks me through a logical thought process that enables me not only to better understand the answer but to see the question better. But it's more than logic. It is a life-giving word that works its transformation beyond the healing of a broken bone or deteriorating organ. Mind, body, and soul receive healing medicine from the hands of Brad Burke. He offers good remedies for searching souls."

—DR. BRIAN C. STILLER
PRESIDENT, TYNDALE UNIVERSITY COLLEGE AND SEMINARY

"Dr. Brad Burke's series is an enormously helpful guide for all who yearn for a personal, intimate relationship with God. His critical analysis of personal spirituality is enlightening; his thoughtful answers to some of our toughest questions are both provocative and compelling; his insights into the rising twenty-first-century generation are perceptive; his medical perspective is fascinating; but most of all, his portrayal of the only true God is profound."

—DR. WILLIAM J. McRAE
PRESIDENT EMERITUS, TYNDALE UNIVERSITY COLLEGE AND SEMINARY

"Doctor Brad's pen is sharper than his scalpel. His stories gripped me from page one. His honest search for answers to the mysteries of miracles, suffering, evil, and the existence of God is not just entertaining, it is immensely helpful and practical."

—PHIL CALLAWAY
SPEAKER, AUTHOR OF *LAUGHING MATTERS*

IS GOD OBSOLETE?

AN M.D. EXAMINES

IS GOD OBSOLETE?

DR. BRAD BURKE

Victor®

The Bible Teacher's Teacher

COOK COMMUNICATIONS MINISTRIES
Colorado Springs, Colorado • Paris, Ontario
KINGSWAY COMMUNICATIONS LTD
Eastbourne, England

Victor® is an imprint of
Cook Communications Ministries, Colorado Springs, CO 80918
Cook Communications, Paris, Ontario
Kingsway Communications, Eastbourne, England

IS GOD OBSOLETE?
© 2006 by Brad Burke

Published in association with the literary agency of Les Stobbe, 300 Doubleday Road, Tryon, NC 28782.

The Web addresses (URLs) recommended throughout this book are solely offered as a resource to the reader. The citation of these Web sites does not in any way imply an endorsement on the part of the author or the publisher, nor does the author or publisher vouch for their content for the life of this book.

Cover Design: Marks & Whetstone
Cover Photo Credit: © BigStockPhoto

First Printing, 2006
Printed in the United States of America

1 2 3 4 5 6 7 8 9 10 Printing/Year 10 09 08 07 06

ISBN-13: 978-0-7814-4280-0
ISBN-10: 0-7814-4280-X

LCCN: 2006922966

To my parents, David and Lucille,
who, by God's grace,
instilled within me a passion
for memorization and
meditation on Scripture

CONTENTS

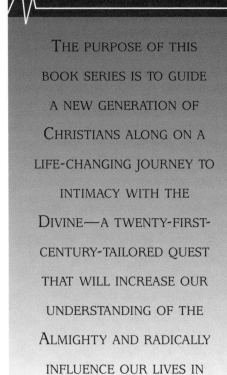

THE PURPOSE OF THIS BOOK SERIES IS TO GUIDE A NEW GENERATION OF CHRISTIANS ALONG ON A LIFE-CHANGING JOURNEY TO INTIMACY WITH THE DIVINE—A TWENTY-FIRST-CENTURY-TAILORED QUEST THAT WILL INCREASE OUR UNDERSTANDING OF THE ALMIGHTY AND RADICALLY INFLUENCE OUR LIVES IN WAYS WE NEVER IMAGINED.

ACKNOWLEDGMENTS

My second career as a writer unexpectedly began in my second year of medical school when I stumbled into the creative world of screenwriting. In a sense, An MD Examines came together remarkably like a major Hollywood film, complete with an executive producer, coproducers, editors, directors, a film studio, a screenwriter—even actors and actresses. Using the film analogy, here are the "rolling credits."

I must begin by thanking my Executive Producer on this extensive project, my Lord and heavenly Father. The astonishing way in which God brought all these talented individuals together blows the fuses in my mind. Whether or not this production wins an Oscar here on earth, God, and God alone, deserves all the glory.

Heather Gemmen, my brilliant producer and content editor, rocks! She enthusiastically presented this project to the studio, Cook Communications. My exceedingly wise coproducer, trusted friend, and mentor for more than twenty-five years, Garry Jenkins, helped steer me clear of false doctrine and "fluff."

IS GOD OBSOLETE?

Craig Bubeck, like an experienced Tinseltown director, finely directed the thematic and visual components of this project at Cook. And the assistant director, Diane Gardner, and film publicist, Michele Tennesen, smoothly coordinated events, meetings, and communiqué between location shoots. There are so many others at Cook who played key roles; I thank them so much for their dedication to spreading God's truth around the world!

Every film needs a good editor. In addition to those mentioned above, Audrey Dorsch worked her own movie magic and brought the scenes together seamlessly.

Script consultants can make or break a film. Several provided valuable advice from scene one to "The End": Garry and Matt Jenkins, Sherri Spence, Dr. Val Jones, Wendy Elaine Nelles, and my parents. God provided other consultants for the production at key times, including world-renowned surgeon and author Dr. Paul Brand.

The Word Guild, the largest Christian writing association in Canada, played the role of a Hollywood talent agency perfectly, bringing together the screenwriter with the editors, producer, script consultant, agent, and even the production company for this powerful movie.

And what's a film without the actors and actresses? My sincere thanks also goes out to all those individuals who brought this film to life by allowing the world to see their inspiring stories.

I am grateful to Les Stobbe, my hardworking agent who helped make this series possible. My heartfelt appreciation also goes to my parents, David and Lucille, whose understanding and support during those tough years when I took a half-decade sabbatical from medicine to write this series ensured my success. I love them both very much.

In almost every film there is a love interest. To Erin, my beautiful wife, I'm looking forward to serving the Lord together for the rest of our lives.

And finally, to my brother Darryl (a stunt coordinator in training) who told me in 1999 that one day I would write a book—and I laughed ...

I apologize.

Introduction

SETTING OUR SIGHTS

I t was the writer and spiritual advisor Thomas à Kempis who once said, "For a small reward a man will hurry away on a long journey, while for eternal life many will hardly take a single step."[1]

Our exhilarating quest into understanding God is a lifelong journey filled with all the eternal and priceless rewards one can possibly imagine! Yet so few people are willing to attempt even a single step. In our day and age, the god of materialism has sidelined the God of the Bible. The god of hedonism and self-centeredness has replaced God our Creator. And the god of our imaginations has made the one true God nearly obsolete in our thinking. Most men and women would rather travel hundreds of miles in search of the worthless "fool's gold" of the world's stuff than take a single step toward the never-ending, unfathomable riches of an intimate relationship with our eternal God.

Some attempt the first step on this important journey but never really get past the front porch. Despite the fact that more resources exist now than at any other time in history—books, tapes, videos, magazines, seminars, and Web sites—countless believers are still searching for a deep-rooted understanding of God. People are desperately seeking truth but instead are being distracted and disillusioned by pop psychology and a watered-down theology. As a result, more believers than ever are frustrated, bitter, discontented,

IT IS IMPERATIVE

THAT WE

ACTUALLY INVITE

GOD ALONG ON

OUR JOURNEY.

and searching for answers that make sense in a world that doesn't. The purpose of this book series is to guide a new generation of Christians along on a life-changing journey to intimacy with the Divine—a twenty-first-century-tailored quest that will increase our understanding of the Almighty and radically influence our lives in ways we never imagined.

Now this may or may not seem obvious to you, but if we ever hope to gain this life-transforming understanding of the one true God on our journey, then it is imperative that we actually *invite God along on our journey*. If you wanted to gain a deep-rooted, intimate understanding of your new bride or groom, you wouldn't trek off on the big honeymoon to Hawaii or the Caribbean and leave your soulmate behind in Bakersfield or Albuquerque!

So I would encourage you to invite God along on this momentous quest. We will venture far beyond the mundane city limits of just a head knowledge of the Divine to attain an exotic, extraordinary *understanding* of our heavenly Father who deeply loves each and every one of us.

But perhaps this isn't why you chose this book. Your appetite or expectations may be somewhat different. Maybe you slid this book off the shelf hoping to find an engaging philosophical debate on the existence of God. If you did, you may be somewhat disappointed.[2] Or perhaps you chose this book series for its intriguing title; needing something to pass the time, you'll allow the words go in one ear and out the other.

INTRODUCTION

There's a chance you didn't even choose this book at all. Maybe a well-meaning friend bought it for you, and rather than insult your pal, you've agreed to read it. So you'll find a comfy couch, some Krispy Kreme doughnuts, and the TV remote, hoping you can skim through the pages during commercials in *Oprah* or the Monday night football game.

But I hope and pray that you've selected this book for a much different reason: I hope that God, working supernaturally in your life, has brought you to the place where you humbly recognize your need of someone bigger than yourself. This need may represent a longing for a personal relationship with your heavenly Father. Or it may symbolize a highly sought-after quest—a lifelong "second honeymoon," so to speak—to develop a more intimate understanding of your Creator and Lord.

If this is your craving—your honest, heartfelt desire—then I invite you to turn the page, and take the first step on this life-changing expedition with me.

Part One

PERSONAL SPIRITUALITY

IS GOD OBSOLETE?

Understanding God, for the dedicated and faithful believer, is a day-by-day, hour-by-hour, mind-, heart-, and soul-grappling journey, yielding priceless and unfathomable treasures … sometimes by the minute … sometimes when the saint is least expecting it.…

1

"MAY I TAKE YOUR ORDER?"

I stood over the limp and bloody body of a sixteen-year-old Hispanic kid—my hand deep inside his chest, massaging his heart.

"Keep going!" barked the chief resident.

I felt the warm muscle slither between my gloved fingers as I squeezed. With so much blood, the boundary between my fingers and the tissue became almost indistinguishable. Nevertheless, everyone in the emergency room knew what I held in my hand.

Months earlier I had crammed my belongings into a couple of suitcases, hopped on a plane, and flown to Los Angeles to begin my surgical residency. From almost the first day of medical school, I had dreamed of becoming a plastic surgeon. Now here was my big chance. Having worked in my parents' small-town jewelry store for eleven summers, repairing watches and intricate jewelry, I felt right at home wielding other fine instruments—namely a scalpel and a needle driver.

IS GOD OBSOLETE?

But my big chance spawned an even bigger challenge: I needed to survive my demanding general surgery rotations (80–115 hour work weeks) at the prestigious Cedars-Sinai Medical Center, a first-class hospital known worldwide for its five-star, round-the-clock care of the rich and famous. Day and night, in a semi jet-lagged state of existence, I cared for a host of sick patients—discovering early on that when disease, suffering, and death come knocking in Tinseltown, absolutely no one is immune.

IN ALL THIS DEATH, SUFFERING, AND HATE— WHERE WAS GOD?

In contrast to our elective surgery cases, in the ER we could never predict the social status of our next trauma victim. The body lying deathly still on the stretcher before me didn't belong to a celebrity. No one knew this kid. The tattoos etched across his now distorted chest identified him with a local gang. But that was it. All we knew was that he had been in the wrong place at the wrong time. A knife thrust deep into his chest had penetrated the heart, severing a vital artery.

It isn't every day that a chest is cracked open in an emergency room—even in LA. No anesthetist. No detailed scrubbing preparation. No time-consuming protocols here. Just a last-ditch, desperate attempt to save a human life.

And yet, despite the frantic hustle around me, the evolving events seemed to be slowing down, unfolding like an old eight-millimeter silent home movie flipped into slow motion. Frame by frame I squeezed his heart—then loosened my grip.

Still, the heart refused to beat.

My mind strayed to the patients I had treated over the previous months. The good-humored, middle-aged businessman: He was exiting a theater one night with his wife when the pair was suddenly blindsided by a mugger who demanded their wallets. Without hesitation, the man quickly relinquished his money—only to be rewarded seconds later with a bullet to the upper face. In the operating room,

I surveyed the bullet's bloody path, wondering what force was responsible for stopping the bullet just millimeters from the frontal lobe of this man's brain.

The wealthy and prominent Hollywood producer: Once powerful and robust in LA's glamour circles, he now struggled to keep down a single morsel of bread in his cancer-ravaged body. There was little I could do.

The polite, twentysomething gay guy with AIDS: He fought for every breath as I stopped by daily to check on the status of the tubes and suctioning device sucking air and bloody fluid out of his weakened chest. I felt sorry that I had to wake him every morning between 5:45 and 6:15 on my rounds. Fortunately, he was one of the last stops on my routine circuit so he got to sleep in more than most of my patients.

The notorious gangbanger: Bullet fragments still embedded in his brain, he miraculously paraded past the hospital rooms of innocent bystanders who had been caught in gang crossfire, and walked out of the hospital; innocent bystanders, some of whom, remained helplessly crippled. Why did we just leave the chunks of lead buried in his brain? There was no reason for us to remove the bullets like you might see in some outlandish, grotesque "B" movie. He was doing quite fine.

Fortune seemed to play favorites with the innocent and the guilty.

The African-American woman in her fifties: She had watched powerlessly as her husband was tied up in their own home and then shot to death. The assailant, apparently out of bullets, grabbed a nearby hammer and repeatedly dented and broke through her skull with the claw end of the metal instrument. Holding a small suction tube, I moved the fine tip delicately through the bloody mess of fragmented bone and tattered brain matter in this woman's head. Despite our best surgical efforts, the woman continued in a vegetative state, later being transferred to a chronic-care facility.

Fortune definitely seemed to play favorites with the innocent and the guilty....

The disjoined eight-millimeter frames continued to roll through my head like a slow-paced movie trailer promoting a dark, demented film.

IS GOD OBSOLETE?

But even as the scenes played out, I was keenly aware of what was happening in this precise moment. Looking past the tattoos and endotracheal tube, I gazed into the still face of the gangster who was really just a lost kid; and as his hope for survival diminished by the second, the questions sneaked into the defenseless places of my heart. *In all this death, suffering, and hate—where was God? What kind of a God would allow evil to bounce helter-skelter from person to person, leaving heartache and death in its path?*

What was God thinking?

IT DOESN'T MATTER WHAT CONTINENT WE CALL HOME, WHAT COLOR OUR SKIN IS, OR WHAT CHURCH, TEMPLE, OR SYNAGOGUE WE ATTEND; SOONER OR LATER WE WILL QUESTION THE ALMIGHTY'S COMPETENCY IN RUNNING THE UNIVERSE.

These pointed questions represent only the crest of a giant tidal wave—a steadily rising wall of questions that keeps growing with every "mile" of time. The triumph of the wicked caused Israel's greatest leader, King David, a man after God's own heart, to cry out, "Why, O Lord, do you stand far off? Why do you hide yourself in times of trouble?" (Ps. 10:1). "Why does your anger smolder against the sheep of your pasture?" (Ps. 74:1b). Similarly, the patriarch Job, famous for his patience, cried out to God, "Why have you made me your target? Have I become a burden to you?" (Job 7:20b). Even Jesus, the Son of God, while hanging on the cross between heaven and earth, uttered the words, *"'Eloi, Eloi, lama sabachthani?'*—which means, 'My God, my God, why have you forsaken me?'"* (Mark 15:34b).

Today the media bombards us with countless reports of tragedies. Victims and bereaved families raise the all-too-familiar question: *Why?*

"MAY I TAKE YOUR ORDER?"

Why would a God of love allow an earthquake to kill more than 50,000 people? Why would he let a tsunami snuff out the lives of more than 150,000 people in one day? Couldn't the Creator of the universe have stopped a simple fuel leak from killing three hundred people aboard a commercial jet? Why can't God prevent a handful of terrorists from killing thousands of people? And why can't our all-powerful sovereign Lord prevent a microscopic AIDS virus from killing millions? If God really exists and has power, why does this tidal wave of questions even exist?

THE RIGHT QUESTIONS

To question God is only human. It doesn't matter what continent we call home, what color our skin is, or what church, temple, or synagogue we attend; sooner or later we will question the Almighty's competency in running the universe.

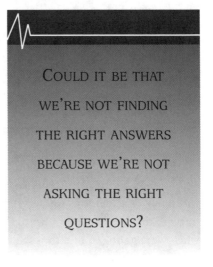

COULD IT BE THAT WE'RE NOT FINDING THE RIGHT ANSWERS BECAUSE WE'RE NOT ASKING THE RIGHT QUESTIONS?

Chances are, your life has already collided with this mighty tidal wave of questions. Maybe you've cried out to God from a church pew, demanding to know why your only child lies at the front in a silk-lined casket. Maybe you've whispered the words from a hospital room, tears streaming down your cheeks as you held your best friend's hand. Or perhaps you've cried yourself to sleep, feeling the empty place beside you where your husband or wife used to lie.

Perhaps you've fought desperately to get around this towering obstacle of questions—but to no avail. Maybe you've given up on God, completely worn down from asking questions that seem to cyclone into even more questions. Your anger has turned to apathy. Your bitterness has been transformed into feelings of helplessness. For you, life is a cruel, twisted maze that keeps changing by the hour, a tortuous maze for which God has seemingly provided no solution—essentially no way out.

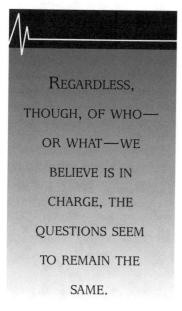

REGARDLESS, THOUGH, OF WHO—OR WHAT—WE BELIEVE IS IN CHARGE, THE QUESTIONS SEEM TO REMAIN THE SAME.

It's easy in discouraging times like these to question and blame our heavenly Father. Many of us grew up hearing the all-too-familiar phrase "God loves you." You may have wondered, *If God loves me so much, why am I suffering? Why can't a loving God shield me from this unbearable pain? Why does he allow people to suffer to the point that they throw up their hands and deny his existence?*

And yet, could it be that we're not finding the right answers because we're not asking the right questions? Do we, as Charles Swindoll points out, make the all-too-common mistake of viewing life from a horizontal perspective when we should be gazing on life from a vertical—a divine—perspective? Do we get so taken up with trying to make sense of life from our restricted viewpoint on earth that we never really step back to see the big picture through the eyes of God in heaven? How can we ask the right questions when we're gazing at life from the wrong perspective?

What's more, we automatically assume that the "right answers" should make sense to absolutely everyone on the planet.

Could it be, though, that our frustration with God's answers—or apparent lack of answers—is because we don't understand the God we're questioning? Do we really have a solid understanding of God's holiness, justice, sovereignty, wisdom, and love? Are we asking the proper questions, from the proper perspective, based on a proper understanding of God?

Maybe not. After all, not everyone questions—or abandons—the same God of Abraham. Some of us believe in a different "force" or, as one writer puts it, "a personification—of life force or society or order or some blend of such personifications."[1] Though approximately 95 percent of Americans would say they "believe in God,"[2] we know that almost 10 percent of those in this category believe in a nameless "higher power"[3] or an aloof "universal spirit." (Fewer than eight in ten Americans believe in a personal heavenly Father who protects us and responds to prayers.)[4]

Regardless, though, of who—or what—we believe is in charge, the questions seem to remain the same. We "instinctively expect"[5] only good from this higher power, as if it were our legitimate cosmic right to perpetually enjoy the "Happy Meals" of life. And when the "cosmic cashier" screws up and slides us something we didn't order, we grow angry and start questioning the cashier's competency—not to mention his intelligence, motives, and dedication in serving us, the "paying customer."

Everyone will, at some point in his or her life, question the universe's cashier. When the questions outnumber the answers, the atheist rationally concludes that God—or this cosmic cashier—doesn't exist. With so many "Happy Meal" orders getting screwed up, how can there possibly be a God?

EVERYONE WILL QUESTION THE UNIVERSE'S CASHIER.

While an atheist believes there is no God, an agnostic, according to the *Columbia Encyclopedia*, "holds that the existence of God cannot be logically proved or disproved."[6] It was the English biologist T. H. Huxley who first invented the word *agnostic* because he was fed up with everyone constantly labeling him an atheist.

Granted, many agnostics nowadays argue that the definition above is shallow and misleading. An agnostic, they assert, can still believe in the existence of the Almighty while believing that "the nature of God is unknown, and probably unknowable."[7] There may be a divine cashier on duty, but we'll probably never know, much less understand, the cashier's nature—and why our Happy Meals don't keep coming.

I've time and again pondered what it must be like for atheists and agnostics, or anyone else for that matter, to traipse through life's convoluted maze without the divine Father by their side. As a

IS GOD OBSOLETE?

child, memorizing Bible verses and attending church every Sunday made it difficult—if not impossible—for me to envision anyone without God.

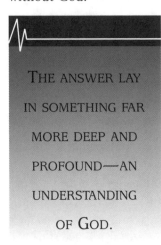

THE ANSWER LAY IN SOMETHING FAR MORE DEEP AND PROFOUND—AN UNDERSTANDING OF GOD.

Recently, I came across the writings of J. I. Packer, a prominent theologian, who argued that traveling through life without God is as "cruel to ourselves" as dropping an "Amazonian tribesman" into London's chaotic Trafalgar Square. "Disregard the study of God," he says, and you will "sentence yourself to stumble and blunder through life blindfold, as it were, with no sense of direction and no understanding of what surrounds you."[8]

But I ask, "Is this analogy particularly fair?" Do atheists, agnostics, and everyone else who rejects the God of Abraham and Isaac really travel through life apprehensive—blundering along with no understanding whatsoever of life's events whizzing past them?

I would have to agree with the ordained minister and theologian J. B. Phillips, who argues that a prevailing wall of ignorance separates those who do not know God from those who claim they do.[9] Just as I will never know what it's like for an atheist or agnostic to live life without God, so too will most atheists and agnostics never know what it's like to walk down life's alleys hand in hand with an intimate and loving heavenly Father. Admittedly, some do find out eventually.

The Oxford and Cambridge Professor C. S. Lewis, once known as a "happy atheist,"[10] embraced God as his Savior when he was about thirty years of age. Later, Lewis became the celebrated Christian author of more than twenty-five books, including the Chronicles of Narnia series. "Few 20th-century figures have more pervasively influenced Christendom than C. S. Lewis," writes Dr. Gerard Reed.[11] And Josh McDowell, a former agnostic who once tried to disprove the resurrection of Jesus Christ, has since authored or coauthored more than seventy-seven books for his Creator. "Few individuals have had as

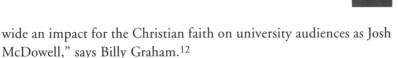
wide an impact for the Christian faith on university audiences as Josh McDowell," says Billy Graham.[12]

In contrast to McDowell, many searching agnostics fail to push the doorbell after arriving at God's doorstep. Blinded by life's tragedies and uncertainties, they ask, "Cannot God [if he exists] treat us as intelligent adults and let us have at least a few hints as to what life is all about?"[13]

Indeed, is this not the same question that nearly *everyone* seems to be asking? Why has God left us here on this earth to fend for ourselves without letting us in on at least some of the mysteries of life?

THE CONTROLLING QUESTION

As my medical career progressed, I discovered that my patients and their families were asking similar questions—but not out loud. They didn't scream down the halls, "GOD! Why am I suffering with pancreatic cancer? I trusted you, and look what you did!" Fathers and mothers didn't stand atop the hospital roof shouting out defiantly, "GOD! Why did you allow my child to be shot in the head? What kind of a God are you anyway?"

They didn't do these things. Instead, they bundled up all their anger, all their frustration and bitterness, and heaved it at the doctors, nurses, and whoever else was involved in their care. I didn't always know who was asking what questions—but I always knew who wasn't getting the answers they were looking for.

Then I made another interesting observation: My most exasperating, most abusive patients, along with their even more abusive families, didn't fall into any particular "God-belief" category. In fact, some of my worst experiences were with those who had supposedly dedicated their lives to God. The pastor would finish praying with the family, say a few encouraging words, and then—walking past the leather Bible on the nightstand—exit the room.

A few minutes later I'd step into the same room, and WHOOSH!—one tomahawk anger missile would come hurtling at me! Often it came via a family member: "The nurse didn't change the bandages yet this morning! The therapists aren't pushing him enough! The therapists were ten minutes late! Why did you prescribe Tylenol without asking me? You ordered the X-ray thirty minutes ago—where is it? The eggs are cold! I ordered scrambled eggs! My father didn't get his eggs!" And so on. I remember one mother who would glare at me every time I set foot in the room, as if I were the one who had pulled the trigger on her fifteen-year-old boy, now disabled.

Fortunately for doctors and the medical community as a whole, the majority of patients don't act this way. Many merely attribute their tragic circumstances to "bad luck," believing that no higher power is responsible for their misfortunes. How can they be angry with God when he isn't even in control?

When I took a closer look at some of my model patients, however, I discovered that they shared a common belief with some of my most demanding patients: a belief that God was definitely in control, allowing whatever tragedy it was to strike. And I wondered: Why such a radical difference in behavior between these two groups of patients? If patients with similar tragedies truly believed that God was in complete control, why were some so incredibly angry with God while others, seemingly, were not?

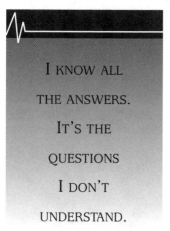

I KNOW ALL THE ANSWERS. IT'S THE QUESTIONS I DON'T UNDERSTAND.

In the years that followed I searched for the answer, and eventually I found it. The answer didn't lie, however, in the power of positive thinking. It didn't lie in education or social status. Nor did it lie in membership to a particular religious denomination. The answer lay in something far more deep and profound—*an understanding of God.*

I'm not talking merely about a head knowledge of the Almighty, but also a deep-rooted, heart-penetrating understanding of God's incomparable character and his sometimes mysterious ways. In essence, one group believed God *owed* them a long life of happiness and health in exchange for their loyalty, and the other group did not.

No doubt my model patients who trusted God were angry. But their anger was not directly rooted in the belief that they deserved only "Happy Meals" from God. Their anger was more a righteous indignation at the wickedness that had deprived them of their health—whether it came via a drunk driver or imperfect genes stemming from Adam and Eve's sin in the Garden of Eden. Anger is not necessarily wrong in and of itself, but the driving force *behind* the anger is what must be carefully analyzed.

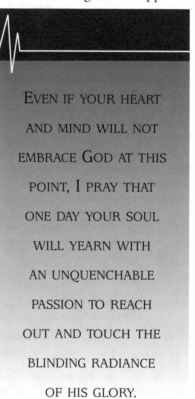

EVEN IF YOUR HEART AND MIND WILL NOT EMBRACE GOD AT THIS POINT, I PRAY THAT ONE DAY YOUR SOUL WILL YEARN WITH AN UNQUENCHABLE PASSION TO REACH OUT AND TOUCH THE BLINDING RADIANCE OF HIS GLORY.

SHRINKING THE TIDAL WAVE

I fondly remember many early childhood visits to my beloved grandparents. My deeply imprinted memories of them are even more cherished now that they are gone. My grandfather was a humble man with a big heart and an even bigger laugh. He loved to repeat jokes and favorite sayings and then laugh as though it were the first time he had ever told them.

Occasionally I would wander into his study; sometimes he was there, sorting through paperwork for his lumber mill, but often he wasn't. I'd curiously meander about the cluttered, dusty room, examining his peculiar collection of timeworn books, paintings, and photographs.

On one such occasion I noticed, just above the doorway, an oval wooden plaque that I had overlooked on previous excursions. I had heard my grandfather laughingly say the words, but this was the first time I had actually set my little eyes on them. In bold black script across the plaque was this maxim:

> I know all the answers.
> It's the questions
> I don't understand.

Thinking back, I believe my grandfather kept the plaque there as a humorous warning to himself—as well as to those who mistakenly thought they knew all the answers. Similarly, I purpose to keep this plaque above the doorway of my mind, lest—in writing this book series—I mislead my readers into thinking that we can know all the answers. I admit straight off that I don't possess all the answers. No one does except God. And anyone who tells you otherwise probably doesn't understand the questions.

Nonetheless, God has certainly left us some valuable truths as to what life is all about; indispensable clues that allow us a deeper, though limited, understanding of his character—and consequently, a deeper understanding of who we are and why we exist. We will attempt to rise above this baffling tidal wave of questions by examining the question "What was God thinking?" but to think that we can reduce centuries of towering questions to a trivial little puddle is foolishly absurd.

I confess that tackling such a mammoth and noble subject as What was God thinking? and trying to contain the material in a few small books will be no easy task. In many ways it's like trying to cram the world-famous 300-acre Royal Botanic Gardens at Kew, containing more than 40,000 kinds of plants, into an average-sized backyard. Sure, you could pick a glorious array of beautiful and exotic plants to fill your little patch, but barely a dent would be made in Britain's lavish garden.

Still, I have carefully selected the most exquisite "plants" (the series subject matter) using two criteria: one, those perfections, or attributes, of God that give rise to the most questions and confusion; and two, those perfections of God that, when firmly grasped in our hearts, will have the greatest impact on our lives.

While I will do my best in this book series to "take your order" by responding to many of your toughest questions about God, I have to forewarn that you may not get exactly what you request. Since gaining a *true* understanding of God is our primary goal, I'm not going to cheat you by serving up a God you may *want*. Instead, I'm going to richly describe and illustrate for you a God you *desperately need*. A God so preciously unique, so utterly radiant, so infinitely wise, so wonderfully loving, and so magnificently holy, that even if your heart and mind will not embrace God at this point, I pray that one day your soul will yearn with an unquenchable passion to reach out and touch the blinding radiance of his glory.

IS GOD OBSOLETE?

We can never know who or what

we are till we know at least

something of what God is.[1]

—A. W. TOZER,
THE KNOWLEDGE OF THE HOLY

2
MAKE A WISH!

I'd be naive, of course, to think that absolutely everyone reading this book genuinely desires a deeper understanding of God. At this very moment this thought may be at the forefront of your mind: "I'm *really* successful. I have a challenging and lucrative career, a wonderful family, perfect health; I couldn't be more happy and content with my life. Why then do I need an *understanding* of God? What's wrong with the basic *knowledge* I possess?"

Consider the following scenario.

It's your birthday. Not just any old birthday, but a real party-time, whoop-it-up bash! Maybe you've just turned a milestone—twenty-five, forty, or sixty-five. Your sweetheart has thrown a cool surprise party for you at one of the hippest restaurants in town. Half the joint is yours—streamers and balloons from ceiling to floor. All your close friends and family are gathered around—enjoying the hors d'oeuvres, laughing, joking, congratulating you on making it this far in life without killing your boss or your neighbor's obnoxious tomcat!

IS GOD OBSOLETE?

Suddenly everyone breaks out into the "Happy Birthday" chorus! The flaming chocolate cake arrives, your darling's arms are around your shoulders, and a big kiss is planted on your cheek. You feel a warm, soft breath in your ear as you hear the words, "Make a wish!"

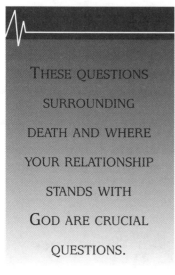

THESE QUESTIONS SURROUNDING DEATH AND WHERE YOUR RELATIONSHIP STANDS WITH GOD ARE CRUCIAL QUESTIONS.

Looking around the room, everything seems so perfect, and you wonder to yourself, *What more could I possibly wish for in life?*

With the night drawing to a close, you say good-bye to the last guest. Your arms are loaded with presents. You and your soul mate stroll down the darkened street, laughing and playfully arguing over who devoured the most chocolate cake. The heated where-to-park-the-car argument that erupted earlier seems so silly now. You realize your partner's purpose in avoiding the valet parking was to buy more time, thereby giving the guests a chance to arrive.

Reaching your Mercedes sedan in the nearly empty parking lot, you fumble with the keys—still laughing and juggling presents. As you lean forward, inserting the key into the door, the top present begins to slide. You grab for it, but the box hits the pavement with a thud.

What happens next is a blur. You remember the piercing scream—maybe it was your own. You remember feeling a sharp pain in your chest. And you remember looking down at your shirt, watching it slowly become soaked with blood. Then you're enveloped by a still blackness.

In the span of a second, your life is altered. A common kitchen knife has entered and exited your chest—all for the sake of the little bit of cash in your wallet. It's no longer the sixteen-year-old Hispanic kid on the emergency room table—it's you. You lie unconscious, your blood-smeared chest cut wide open, with a doctor you've never met standing over you, squeezing your warm, motionless heart. Minutes later you're rushed up to the operating room. The doctors work feverishly, trying their best to repair the severed artery and muscle, just like they did for the Hispanic kid.

But, alas, too much time has expired. Looking up at the clock, the anesthetist notes the time and writes it in your chart: *Time of death: 11:23 p.m.*

If you could have somehow predicted this tragic ending to your birthday (like the tragic ending to the life of the sixteen-year-old Hispanic kid), what would you have wished for earlier? Would you have wished you had lived your life differently? Would you have wished that somehow you could have uncovered your purpose in life? Would your wish have revolved around your missed opportunity for an intimate relationship with the God who created you?

In this day and age, only the morbid (and some writers and forensic pathologists) spend their days intrigued with tragic endings and death. For most of the world, death is seen as the painful end of life's roller-coaster journey—the mysterious beginning of yet another. Consequently, many block out the idea of death without ever giving a serious thought to Jesus' words in Matthew's gospel: "What good will it be for a man if he gains the whole world, yet forfeits his soul?" (Matt. 16:26a). Perhaps you've seen the T-shirt: "He who dies with the most toys *still dies.*"

HAVE YOU EVER PAUSED FOR EVEN A SECOND TO CONTEMPLATE WHO CONTROLS YOUR SOUL'S DESTINY?

These questions surrounding death and where your relationship stands with God, the judge and creator of the universe, are *crucial* questions. They cannot simply be tossed into the not-so-nice-things-to-think-about box. We will all stand before God on the final day to give an account of our lives. What will the answer from your lips be?

IS GOD OBSOLETE?

Right now you might be lounging around on your comfy porch, admiring the world in your backyard; yet have you ever stopped to consider who owns the property? Have you ever taken a moment in the clamor of life to quietly consider these important questions: *Who created me? Who owns my life? Why was I created?* Have you ever paused for even a second to contemplate who controls your soul's destiny?

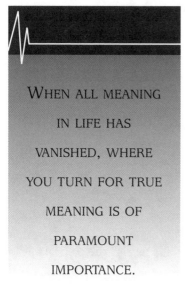

WHEN ALL MEANING IN LIFE HAS VANISHED, WHERE YOU TURN FOR TRUE MEANING IS OF PARAMOUNT IMPORTANCE.

You might wonder where we can find the answers to these important questions. Don't you think that if an all-powerful and wise God exists, he would want to communicate his truth to us by the most objective means possible? Wouldn't someone as intelligent as God write down these answers for us in black and white—in the number-one best-selling book of all time? Perhaps he has already told us what he was thinking.

After tragically losing all his sons, daughters, servants, and possessions, Job confessed from the ashes that in God's "hand is the soul of every living thing, and the breath of all mankind" (Job 12:10 KJV). We spend more time reading the fine print in our life insurance policies than we do the large print in our Bibles. As a result, many are truly uninsured when disaster strikes.

Insurance certainly does have its advantages. Heaven forbid, though, that I should mislead you into fancying that God is merely an underwriter for our soul's insurance policy that we cash in when we die. If this were God's intention, he would have inspired a slew of lawyers to draft up detailed legal forms—not forty-plus common writers to pen the Bible. No, God had a much broader aim when he inspired the writing of his Word.

Consider a second scenario.

MAKE A WISH!

Let's suppose it wasn't you on the stretcher that the paramedics wheeled in. Perhaps—like the best friend of the sixteen-year-old stabbing victim, whom I spoke with later—you watched the knife go in. You're all alone, slumped next to the pay phone in the hushed hospital corridor. Consumed with guilt, you wonder if you could have somehow prevented what happened. Your loved one lies on the operating room table, and at this heartrending moment, nothing else matters. You try praying, but it's your first real talk with God. Awkwardly, you cry out, "God, please spare his (or her) life! I promise I'll go to church every Sunday. I'll be a better person, I swear. I don't love him (or her) like I should. But please, oh God, just one more chance, one more chance … I beg you…."

Through your tears you notice two feet appear. Up to this point you've tried to maintain a brave demeanor. But now everything falls apart. Looking up into the surgeon's face, you realize that you will never get that chance. There will be no more birthday parties. No more laughing and joking. And no more late-night strolls with your soul mate.

At first you deny it, hoping you'll soon snap out of this cruel dream. But eventually the anger and guilt take over … and from here on, your life will be forever changed.

ELIMINATING THE RUST

I have witnessed such devastating life transformations many times. The passing away of husbands, wives, children, and friends creates trails of bitterness and remorse that loved ones seem intent on following until their own sometimes premature deaths. Often these ruinous emotions culminate in an agonizing life of psychosomatic illness fueled by "what ifs" and "how comes." When all meaning in life has vanished, where you turn for true meaning is of paramount importance. Turn to alcohol, drugs, gambling, or sex, and the results can be disastrous.

I realize that for some of you, such unforeseen tragedies have never arrived in life's mailbox. Life's pleasures just keep piling up unexpectedly at your door, instilling within you a false sense of security—perhaps causing you to entirely dismiss your need for a personal God and Savior.

But let me ask you this, dear friend: Deep down in your innermost being, *are you truly happy and content with your life?* Are you able to richly enjoy life's finest pleasures to the fullest? Have all the company stocks, mansions, properties, yachts, and cars you've accumulated in life delivered the enduring contentment you've longed for? Or is your happiness and contentment merely a coat of paint you've meticulously brushed over the rust on your mailbox—the troubles and anxieties of your soul—fooling your neighbors into believing that your life is a smooth, gleaming metal without a spot of corrosion? Merely *exhibiting* happiness and contentedness, and actually *possessing* a true inner peace and joy are two completely different things. Sooner or later the rust on your mailbox will eat through, necessitating that you find some more paint.

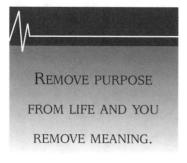

REMOVE PURPOSE FROM LIFE AND YOU REMOVE MEANING.

But praise God that the joy and the peace that bountifully flow from his abundant warehouse don't just cover the rust—*they eliminate it!* Our God is the "Father of compassion and the God of all comfort, who comforts us in all our troubles," writes the apostle Paul (2 Cor. 1:3–4). Not the God of *some* comfort, but the God of *all* comfort! To those who love him, God promises a fulfilling joy and an unspeakable peace "which transcends all understanding"—regardless of the circumstances (Phil. 4:7; cf. Ps. 16:11; Rom. 15:13).

Perhaps, though, your relaxed lifestyle, made possible by some wise financial choices on your part, has fooled you into thinking you possess this deep peace from God. If so, this next question may uncover some hidden rust: Have you discovered *true* meaning in life? If I were to offer you *one year* of all-out hedonism, jam-packed with all the promiscuous sex, alcohol, cocaine, wealth, power, and celebrity status you could possibly wish for, you might turn it all down for the laid-back life you now enjoy. But could you still say that your life has *real* meaning? If I offered you instead an eternity—trillions and trillions of "years"—of indescribable joy, happiness, contentment, peace, and meaning in a right relationship with God, would you also turn this down? In relation to eternity, the pursuit of a hedonistic, self-centered, or comfortable lifestyle is a mere minute of meaningless madness.

THERE ISN'T ONE THING WE DO IN LIFE THAT IS NOT INFLUENCED IN SOME WAY BY OUR IMPRESSION OF GOD.

Hundreds of millions on our planet are trying to understand or "discover" themselves in the context of such a pleasure-cruise life. But how many will actually find what they spend their fleeting lives searching for? Even those who confess to be pursuing God do not always find true meaning. Every cult and religious denomination carries with it a subgroup of followers who are passionately searching for real meaning in life—whether they be Hare Krishnas, Jehovah's Witnesses, or born-again Christians.

For example, a survey completed by two of America's most respected pollsters, George Barna and George Gallup Jr., showed that "35 percent of born-again Christians say they are still searching for meaning in life." Ironically, a similar percentage of non-Christians admit the same thing.[2]

Ravi Zacharias, the apologetics scholar and popular speaker, declares, "Purpose is to life what the skeleton is to the body."[3] Remove purpose from life, and you remove the very framework of your goals, aspirations, and passions. Remove purpose from life and you remove meaning. How can one truly understand his or her purpose in this world without having a decent understanding of the Purpose-giver?

All this leads me to wonder: *How well does the average person understand God and his will for his or her life?*

IS GOD OBSOLETE?

LIKE NOTHING ELSE

While associate professor at Dallas Theological Seminary, Dr. Robert P. Lightner wrote, an "understanding of [God] provides a basis for understanding one's self and one's responsibility before God and other man."[4] The Swiss Protestant reformer John Calvin rightly testified "that man never attains to a true self-knowledge until he have [sic] previously contemplated the face of God, and come down after such contemplation to look into himself."[5] St. Augustine wrote in his *Confessions,* "Thou hast made us for thyself and restless is our heart until it comes to rest in thee."[6]

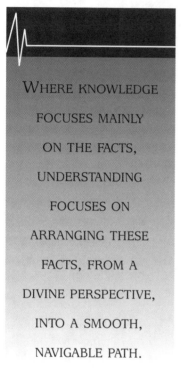

WHERE KNOWLEDGE FOCUSES MAINLY ON THE FACTS, UNDERSTANDING FOCUSES ON ARRANGING THESE FACTS, FROM A DIVINE PERSPECTIVE, INTO A SMOOTH, NAVIGABLE PATH.

Before we can recognize and deal with our deep-rooted pride, injustice, and folly, we must first examine the majestic, just, and holy character of our perfect Creator.[7] In order to understand something of our designated role here on earth, it is important that we first understand the God who gives these roles. Before we can attain true rest, we must first come with a humble heart to the one true Rest-giver. Without an understanding of God and his priorities, "everything else in the Bible and in life," declares Lightner, "becomes hazy and meaningless."[8]

It was A. W. Tozer who wrote, "What comes into our minds when we think about God is the most important thing about us."[9] This is so true. How we view God influences how we treat others, how we handle ourselves in moral situations, how we perceive and handle adversity, how we manage success and failure, and how we introspectively view ourselves. All our actions, thoughts, aspirations, attitudes, beliefs, and future plans are profoundly colored by our perception of the Almighty. *There isn't one thing we do in life that is not influenced in some way by our impression of God.*

"Tell me what a person believes," says Ralph Waldo Emerson, "and I'll tell you what he'll do."[10] Tell me your understanding of God, and I'll predict how you'll react in life's moral arena. Consequently, how you handle yourself in tragedy directly reflects who's in control of your life, along with what you understand to be true—the very core of your being.

So I ask a final time, "Why do we need an understanding of God?" An understanding of God gives us true inner peace and confidence in where our immortal souls stand in his sight. It also provides a direct avenue to finding true meaning in life—even in the midst of hardship and tragedy. In addition, an understanding of God allows us a better understanding of ourselves, along with fresh insight into our divinely appointed roles here on earth. But most importantly, an understanding of God leads to a deeper, richer, and far more fulfilling relationship with him, our Lord and heavenly Father. That's why having a basic knowledge of God just doesn't cut it. It's the difference between just reading about someone in the newspaper and actually living with that person in a close relationship. Only by understanding God can we genuinely experience his presence and uncover true meaning and purpose in life.

In sum, nothing will so greatly affect your life and change your outlook on the world as an intimate understanding of God and his ways.

ARRANGING OUR STEPPING-STONES

Picture yourself standing precariously on the edge of a churning, one-hundred-foot-wide river. Gazing across the surging waters, you spy some haphazardly spaced, two-foot-wide stepping-stones—representing your *only* hope of making it across alive. And you must make it across!

You're a little hesitant to proceed, though, because the stones appear in short supply. "Ahh, what the heck," you finally say. With more determination than a one-legged cockroach stranded in a light-bulb testing facility, you focus your eyes and energy on a nearby slippery rock, grit your teeth, and jump—just barely making it. Whew!

After regaining your balance and courage, you glance around for your next rock, spying one about four feet away. Head down, focusing hard, you leap again, this time landing wildly off balance—almost slipping off the moss-covered stone. But now the closest rock ahead will require a giant seven-foot leap! Rather than risk it, you backtrack a bit, choosing a closer stone to your right.

So you jump to fifteen different stones—only to discover that you've taken the wrong route and must backtrack.

After an exhaustive hour of zigzagging back and forth across the treacherous water, you realize that the situation is hopeless, and you return to your starting position on the riverbank, frustrated and fatigued.

A similar maddening experience occurs in our minds almost every day. These stepping-stones represent the God facts in our consciousness, and the wide chasm is the exasperating, intellectual question you are trying to navigate. When it comes to understanding God, there are many daunting rivers—or mental hurdles—in our minds, such as, *Why doesn't God prove himself to the world? What is God's will for my life? Why does God allow so much suffering on our planet? Why doesn't God perform more miracles today? Why does God allow evil to exist? Why did God allow my loved one to die?* And so forth.

UNDERSTANDING IS MUCH MORE ABOUT WHO WE ARE THAN WHAT WE APPEAR TO BE.

In trying to cross these often demoralizing rivers, you will likely focus all your mental energy on only a few facts, or stepping-stones, at a time (e.g., God is all-powerful or God is a loving Father). If the river is relatively narrow (a small mental hurdle), then there's a decent chance you'll make it safely across on your stepping-stones—even if they are sort of haphazardly placed.

But if the river is extremely wide, representing a really tough question about God, then chances are these stepping-stones will fail you in your endeavor; this means another exasperating chasm remains untraversed in your logic. The more often you attempt to cross the obstinate river, the more frustrated you will grow. For many atheists and agnostics, all it takes is one uncrossable river and God is given the big heave-ho.

> UNDERSTANDING INHABITS THE DEEPEST RECESSES OF OUR HEARTS AND ACTS AS THE GATEKEEPER OF OUR SOULS.

But imagine yourself at the controls of a giant, two-hundred-foot tall crane. Skillfully pushing the levers and buttons of the powerful rig, you carefully lift each stepping-stone out of the water, gently repositioning it in line with other stones. Where *knowledge* focuses mainly on the facts, *understanding* focuses on *arranging* these facts, from a divine perspective, into a smooth, navigable path. When all the stepping-stones are neatly in place, no longer are you forced to "kill yourself" focusing on each solitary stone. Rather than erratic leaps from one stone to the next, the journey becomes a safe, confident, and smooth stride across the river. To *understand* (the verb) is to arrange these stepping-stones to form a level pathway on our journey across these perplexing rivers. *Understanding* (the noun) is the life-changing prize you gain in the process—the treasures of understanding uncovered.

This is the number one reason that everyone has a different "God mosaic." (A mosaic is a collection of colorful pieces fit together like a puzzle to form a design.) *Knowledge* entails finding the vibrant pieces for the mosaic; understanding involves ingeniously fitting all the pieces together. For some believers, their pieces decently fit to form a fairly coherent and recognizable mosaic. But for others, their mosaics are like a thousand puzzle pieces randomly thrown into a pail of glue. The pieces may all be there, and they may all be stuck together, but the mosaic is so higgledy-piggledy that it only serves to further confuse its owner.

John Locke V said this:

> The understanding, like the eyes, while it makes us see and perceive all things, takes no notice of itself, and it requires art and pains to set it at a distance and make it its own subject.[11]

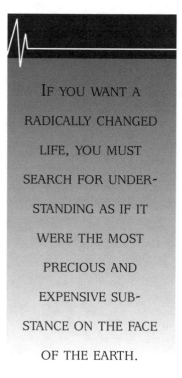

IF YOU WANT A RADICALLY CHANGED LIFE, YOU MUST SEARCH FOR UNDERSTANDING AS IF IT WERE THE MOST PRECIOUS AND EXPENSIVE SUBSTANCE ON THE FACE OF THE EARTH.

Indeed, understanding is the eyes through which we view life. It's the power to discern, absorb, and appreciate the intricate, behind-the-scenes tools that shape our existence. It's the ability to turn the intangible into the tangible. In contrast to intelligence, personality, and social status, understanding is much more about *who* we are than *what* we appear to be. It is the key determinant in how we perceive our surroundings, how we approach complex problems, how we make tough decisions, how we handle criticism, how we view others, and, most importantly, how we view God. Understanding enables us to have an overall view of the bigger picture, granting us the ability to sort out the intangibles of life. Like a skilled stonemason, understanding painstakingly aligns and realigns the facts about God in our minds until we are comfortable with our beliefs. Most important, though, understanding inhabits the deepest recesses of our hearts and acts as the gatekeeper of our souls. Only that which agrees with our God mosaic is allowed entrance to the core of our beings.

As we have seen, the difference between *knowing* and *understanding* is vast. Most of us collect puzzle pieces about God—from books, conversations, seminars, sermons, and even from reading the Bible. But we tend to isolate God's attributes from each other and never successfully tie them all together to adequately demonstrate how they function simultaneously. Yet it is impossible to *truly* understand God unless one is able to see the big picture from God's perspective. To answer the tough tidal wave of questions, one *must* be able to effectively fit together the puzzle pieces of God's eternity, transcendence, wisdom, justice, patience, wrath, holiness, love, sovereignty, and majesty. Truly *knowing God,* then, is much more than just rote head knowledge—or even a basic understanding. *It is a personal understanding that combines all kinds of knowing.* I once heard a wise medical doctor say, "God is not a subject to be learned; he's a person to be known."[12] Genuinely *knowing God* involves a personal, deep-rooted, one-of-a-kind relationship. Even better is an understanding of God that takes us much further than head knowledge. As in marriage, true intimacy is contingent upon understanding your partner's unique character, so too in our cherished relationship with God.

In this book series I provide you with a number of facts—or stepping-stones—about God. My aim, however, is not to merely toss out these stepping-stones like giant Frisbees, but also to help you figure out how to arrange them.

As we travel along on our journey, keep this analogy in the forefront of your mind. Don't focus solely on the stepping-stones I provide, but concentrate on trying to fit the stones together. I've spent thousands of hours studying and meditating on Scripture in an attempt to uncover the correct stepping-stones. To help you align these stones, I've packed as many creative illustrations and analogies into the pages of this book series as possible. You'll find some to be humorous, some touching, some heart wrenching, and many thought provoking. I want to help you succeed.

IS GOD OBSOLETE?

But there is one thing I can't do. I can't actually arrange the stepping-stones in your mind. That part of the journey is up to you. And that's hard work. King Solomon, the wisest man who ever lived (see 1 Kings 3:12), wrote, "Tune your ears to wisdom, and concentrate on understanding. Cry out for insight and understanding. Search for them as you would for lost money or hidden treasure" (Prov. 2:2–4 NLT).

If you want a life-changing understanding of God, you have to cry out for it with every cell in your body. If you want a radically changed life, you must search for understanding as if it were the most precious and expensive substance on the face of the earth. If you don't try your best to arrange the stepping-stones in your mind, someone will try to do it for you. And the results, more often than not, will be disastrous because we are living in a time when many false teachers are merely "tickling" the ears of their students with words they want to hear (see 2 Tim. 4:3).

You must succeed on this journey at all costs!

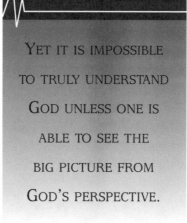

Yet it is impossible to truly understand God unless one is able to see the big picture from God's perspective.

IS GOD OBSOLETE?

How much better to get wisdom than gold,
to choose understanding rather than silver!
—KING SOLOMON
PROVERBS 16:16

3
THE TEN-MILLION-DOLLAR QUESTION

Men and women frequently joke about the troubles they encounter in relationships with the opposite sex. *Men Are from Mars, Women Are from Venus* has become a very popular book. Relationship experts like Gary Smalley tell us that understanding is actually the key to an intimate marriage relationship. When it comes to our relationship with God, some might wonder, "Are we even in the same galaxy?" Why does it often feel that God is on Mars and we are stuck millions of miles away on Venus? Are we really able to connect with our Creator in a meaningful and intimate way? If intimacy demands understanding, can we actually understand our heavenly Father—or will we just *know* him like we might a casual acquaintance we bump into every couple weeks at the gym? Is it even *possible* for us as finite, mortal beings to understand the infinite character of almighty God? Why spend hours reading a series of books on understanding God if it's impossible to actually *comprehend* our Creator?

IS GOD OBSOLETE?

The philosopher Sir William Hamilton would have laughed at the thought. Throughout his life, Sir William boldly asserted that God "is not only inconceivable, but incogitable"[1] and "To think that God is, as we can think Him to be is blasphemy."[2] Now, you may not fully agree with Sir William; you may believe we can know at least

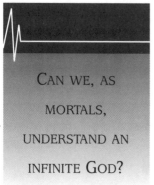

CAN WE, AS

MORTALS,

UNDERSTAND AN

INFINITE GOD?

something about God; but to say that we can actually *understand him?* C'mon, show me the proof!

In our search for the answer, let's consider a third scenario—a much happier one than the first two.

Imagine, for a moment, that it's the year 2020 and you're sitting in the hot seat of the greatest game show in the history of television. It is broadcasted throughout most of the world in twenty-two languages, and the show's ratings have skyrocketed through the roof. And at this moment, the eyes of almost a billion people fall on you. It's the richest, most bizarre game show ever concocted—'cause you're playing for ten million dollars and your teammates are all long dead.

You say, "Wait just a minute! My teammates are all dead? What kind of a messed-up game show is this, anyway?"

Seated at titanium monitors before you are five dead teammates. Technically they're dead, but super-computers have brought them back to life as extraordinarily detailed holograms—thinking, talking, and acting just as they did when they walked the earth. (The characters, some dead for several centuries, have been brought up-to-date in history. Sometimes, though, they short-circuit, stumbling over the modern technology and lingo.) Their sole purpose in this bizarre game show is to guide you to the right answer—that is, if their combative personality quirks can be controlled.

So far you've done remarkably well. The people in the crowd are on their feet, cheering wildly, and you're bouncing up and down for joy because you've just won five million dollars! Imagine the hydrogen turbo-charged Ferrari you could buy with that dough!

THE TEN-MILLION-DOLLAR QUESTION

Trying to calm yourself, you draw in a few deep breaths. The audience gradually sits down—though they remain on the edge of their seats. The game show host, a handsome, commanding man in a glimmering suit, swivels back to you. In a spirited, gung-ho voice, inspiring you with confidence, he asks, "Are you ready for the next question?"

You nod your head, and the familiar drum prelude begins.

"For ten million dollars, here is your last question."

With your palms already sweating, you look down at the monitor:

Question: Can we, as mortals, understand an infinite God?

Answers:

A. Definitely not

B. Somewhat

C. Completely

D. No one knows

A scoffing snicker arises from your third teammate, Madalyn Murray O'Hair, the famous atheist who died mysteriously in the later half of the 1990s.

Ignoring her, you turn to teammate number one, spying the short, willowy frame of the great Immanuel Kant—the eighteenth-century German philosopher and astronomer. His voice, though feeble, brims with conviction; his English is remarkably good.

"A thing in itself cannot be known, save what our minds make it to be. We must believe in God, but our understanding is a false understanding predicated on what our minds tell us." Glancing down at the answers on his monitor he appears deep in thought. "I would choose 'A'—definitely not."

Noting some hesitancy in his answer, you probe, "Are you sure?"

Kant's eyes remain glued to the monitor. "Remote chance it could be 'D'—no one knows. But I would stick with 'A.'"

Somewhat satisfied, you swivel twenty degrees to your second teammate. Dressed in an elaborately embroidered dhoti draped neatly about his hunched body is the Indian philosopher Siddhārtha Gautama, more commonly known as Buddha (fifth century BC). At first glance, he appears to be asleep. Maybe dead. But then you realize he's only meditating.

"Ahh, Mr. Gautama?"

Slowly he raises his head and shoulders in your direction. Overcome that you are actually speaking with the famous Buddha, you half stumble over the syllables. "D-do you think we mortals can understand God?"

A few seconds pass before his brow puckers. "Do gods exist?" he asks softly. "To say they do not exist would be an unwise assumption. But to say a personal God exists would be equally unwise. The universe functions by natural order—not by divine decree." Reflecting some more, he adds, "I cannot know with absolute certainty, but the most sensible answer would be the first—definitely not."

Suddenly, a shrill voice blares out, "Well, I do know with absolute certainty!"

Perched behind her monitor like a cantankerous rooster is Madalyn Murray O'Hair. At one time she was named the most hated woman in America. Disillusioned by Bible stories demonstrating God's wrath, she converted to atheism as a teenager. Now, in her hologram age of fifty, she hasn't changed a bit.

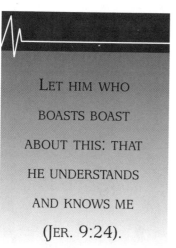

LET HIM WHO BOASTS BOAST ABOUT THIS: THAT HE UNDERSTANDS AND KNOWS ME (JER. 9:24).

"This is a no-brainer!" she snaps. "Anyone with a few neurons still left in their cerebral cortex would have to admit the answer is 'A'—definitely not! How can you understand someone who doesn't even exist?"

Without thinking, you ask, "Are you sure?"

"Of course I'm sure!" she yells back. "Do I look like I'm not sure?"

THE TEN-MILLION-DOLLAR QUESTION

Dropping your head you mumble, "My apologies, Ms. Murray O'Hair."

"Apology accepted!"

Shifting your eyes, you spy big grins spread across the creased faces of your two remaining teammates. Your fourth teammate looks surprisingly spry for someone who is just over 2,600 years old. With a long white beard, flowing white hair, and loose-fitting robe, the aged prophet Jeremiah sits relaxed in his chair. Responding to your body language, Jeremiah takes his cue.

"When I was a kid," he exclaims, stroking his matted beard, "people would boast about their gold palaces and the thousands of sheep and cattle they owned. Nowadays, they boast about those smoke-spewing, horseless chariots that—"

"Automobiles, you idiot!"

Jeremiah nods. "Automobiles. Thank you, Madalyn."

Turning back to you, he continues, "They boast about their automobiles, their beachfront homes, and their funny-looking golden statue awards. But God said 'Let him who boasts boast about this: that he understands and knows me' (Jer. 9:24a). I don't think it is 'C'—completely—so I would pick 'B'—we can understand God somewhat."[3]

Again you ask, "Are you sure?"

"Very sure," replies Jeremiah, "because it was God who told me so."

"Yeah, right!" chimes Madalyn.

Turning, Jeremiah bellows, "Put a straitjacket on your tongue, Madalyn!"

Madalyn screams back, "No, YOU put a straitjacket on YOUR tongue you decrepit little fossil—"

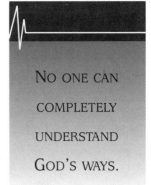

NO ONE CAN COMPLETELY UNDERSTAND GOD'S WAYS.

The host quickly hits a red panic button on the console—resetting all the holograms and promptly restoring peace and quiet.

He looks up, sighing in relief. "Thank goodness for the button!"

The audience laughs as you shift your focus to your last teammate.

IS GOD OBSOLETE?

Exhaling deeply, you say, "I think I could use your help on this one, Solomon."

Born about 350 years before Jeremiah, the renowned King Solomon definitely appears the oldest and wisest of all your teammates. When God granted Solomon one wish, the young king at the age of twenty asked for wisdom and understanding to lead his people. As a result, God gave him a "wise and understanding heart"—greater than anyone who had lived or ever would live. And because Solomon did not selfishly ask for riches and honor, God gave these to him anyway, making Solomon the richest king of his era (1 Kings 3:4–15).

Today Solomon is decked out in a fine purple robe with elaborately engraved gold chains around his neck. He appears to be a little bored—as though we're not making him think hard enough. Folding his arms, he leans back and glances over nonchalantly.

"I agree with Madalyn."

A gasp goes out from the crowd. You do a double take. So does Madalyn.

Solomon's eyes wander about the stage. He seems to be admiring the modern steel architecture and elaborate lighting system. After several seconds, he continues, "I agree with Madalyn—that this question is a no-brainer."

A soft chortle rolls out of Jeremiah.

Pausing for a brief moment, though, Solomon's eyebrows meet in a frown. "Some of my colleagues used to say they could understand God completely. The fools! They couldn't even understand the path of the wind, let alone understand the God who created the wind! No one can completely understand God's ways. Not even me!" (Eccl. 8:16–17; 11:5).

The stage becomes deathly quiet. Everyone, including Madalyn, appears awestruck over Solomon's authoritative presence and wisdom. You squirm in your seat, stumbling again over your next words: "Ah, K-king S-solomon? W-what answer then would you pick?"

Shifting his eyes toward you, he replies, "'B'—we can understand God somewhat—as much as our finite minds will allow."

Not even bothering to ask if he's sure, you glance over to the host, who remarks, "You can leave now with five million dollars, or you can risk it all for a chance at ten million. What is your decision?"

Something inside of you urges you on. Impulsively, you blurt out, "I will choose 'B'—we can understand God somewhat."

Madalyn, Siddhartha, and Immanuel just roll their eyes. Jeremiah and King Solomon nod their approval.

With a questioning stare, the host asks, "Is that your final answer?"

"That's my final answer."

"For ten million dollars, is the answer 'B'?"

The next second seems like an eternity.

Suddenly the monitor starts flashing—and the game show host yells, "YOU'VE JUST WON TEN MILLION DOLLARS!!"

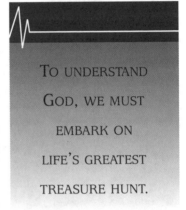

TO UNDERSTAND GOD, WE MUST EMBARK ON LIFE'S GREATEST TREASURE HUNT.

You jump up screaming as hundreds of balloons and streamers drop from the ceiling. The audience goes crazy! The sound is deafening! And the balloons just keep falling! With TV cameras coming at you from all directions, and with a whopping check in your hand, you can't help but scream and shout for joy! You've worked all your life for sixty thousand a year. Now you have made ten million in just one hour! And best of all, you don't have to share it with your teammates— because they're all dead!

You hug the host, the producer, the cameraman, and some little old lady in a red polka-dot dress who jumped past security.

Finally, it's time for you to exit the stage with your ten-million-dollar check. As you're walking past, Solomon leans over, whispering softly in your ear, "Search for it as for hidden treasure" (Prov. 2:4).

You frown, thinking, *I already have the treasure. What's he talking about?*

IS GOD OBSOLETE?

Security hustles you right along, but Solomon shouts out now, "Whatever you do, don't give up searching for it!"

You yell back, "Searching for what?" But Solomon offers no answer.

In a desperate attempt to uncover the truth, you break away from security and dash back out of breath.

THE DIVINE TREASURE FAR SURPASSES OUR WILDEST IMAGINATION.

"Don't give up searching for what?"

Solomon points to the console with his eyes. There, sitting on the corner edge, is a tiny compact disk. "You'll need this," he whispers.

"For what?"

But before he can utter another sound, Solomon's image begins to fade and then suddenly vanishes with the other holograms. With security tugging on one arm, you reach over with the other, grab the disk, and hide it in your pocket.

The security escort stays with you all the way to your waiting stretch limo. The door opens automatically, allowing you entrance into the luxurious leather-seated interior.

All alone now in the back, you can hardly believe what transpired. You've just won ten million dollars! The limo may be doing the speed limit, but your mind is racing along at a hundred miles an hour just thinking of all the ways you can spend the cash.

Then you remember the compact disk. Spying a digital player next to a bottle of champagne, you remove the disk from your pocket and insert it into the slot. Sinking back into the plush seat, you stare down at the player, not quite sure what to expect.

Suddenly, a deep voice grabs your ears. Jerking your head sideways, you discover miniature speakers built into the headrest, from which emanates Solomon's enchanting voice.

> Celebrate for now, but savor one thing,
> That which you have won, you won't need to bring,

THE TEN-MILLION-DOLLAR QUESTION

> For it can't be sold, lost, traded, nor bought,
> It can't be taken, though many have fought,
> So trade that mask for true comprehending,
> Clean out the cobwebs, shed aura and wing,
> 'Cause there's just one map to the treasure sought,
> Choose the wrong map, friend, and suffer your lot.[†]

Although exciting to dream about, the chances of your actually winning ten million dollars on a TV game show are almost nil. But let's imagine, for just a moment, that God visited you one night. And as he did for Solomon, he gave you one wish—anything you wanted, you name it, and it would be yours. If you had just one wish, what would it be? Would you wish for ten million dollars? Would you wish for a long and healthy life filled with all the delectable pleasures your mind could possibly imagine? Or like Solomon, would you push all these fleeting riches aside and wish instead for a wise and understanding heart?

What would your wish be?

Solomon's soft whisper, "Search for it as for hidden treasure," should direct our focus (Prov. 2:4). And this is precisely the direction, or quest, we will undertake in the pages of this book and the books to come. True intimacy with God is possible only if we first *understand God* in the context of a right relationship with his Son, Jesus Christ. To understand God, we must embark on life's greatest treasure hunt. In various ways, it is like any other quest: We'll need a

---

[†] In the last chapter of each book in this series we'll unravel the relevant portion of Solomon's Clues for some practical and vital insight into understanding God. These are fictional clues based on biblical truths. Yet these aren't the only clues Solomon provides. Count on many more to come!

These clues will help us to understand better the five levels of intimacy that are possible with our heavenly Father. You've never heard of these five levels before in this context, but they will make perfect sense. If you find yourself stuck on the first couple of rungs, discovering your own level will help you move up the intimacy ladder. It will also give you a whole new appreciation for what it means to be truly "intimate" with God. This is not just a book series to try and figure out in a curious manner what is going through God's mind; this is a heart-thumping, life-changing journey to intimacy with the Divine.

trusty map, some indispensable tools and supplies, some helpful clues, and of course, lots of determination, courage, and wisdom to spot the true paths, avoid the pitfalls, and overcome the obstacles.

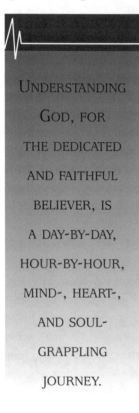

UNDERSTANDING GOD, FOR THE DEDICATED AND FAITHFUL BELIEVER, IS A DAY-BY-DAY, HOUR-BY-HOUR, MIND-, HEART-, AND SOUL- GRAPPLING JOURNEY.

In other ways, though, this grand treasure hunt is unlike any other. The divine treasure far surpasses our wildest imagination: There is more than enough for every believer; the spiritual rewards far exceed our highest expectations; and best of all, we can enjoy these marvelous riches for all of eternity!

You might wonder if this is a pot-of-gold-at-the-end-of-the-rainbow type of hunt. Fortunately for us, it isn't. As we learned from Solomon and Jeremiah in the illustration above, we can understand God somewhat—as much as our finite minds will allow. On the other hand, one can never attain that elusive and mythical "pot of gold" everyone talks about.

Furthermore, "understanding God somewhat" is obviously not an "all-or-nothing" commodity that you either possess or you don't. This is not an Indiana Jones high-flying adventure where you trek off to some exotic jungle, grab your mysterious treasure, and then run like the dickens back home to enjoy your prize. Understanding God, for the dedicated and faithful believer, is a day-by-day, hour-by-hour, mind-, heart-, and soul-grappling journey yielding priceless and unfathomable treasures ... sometimes by the minute ... sometimes when the saint is least expecting it.

Be assured, this is no ordinary treasure hunt.

I'd like to end this chapter with the words of Solomon, the wise king who had all the gold, silver, ivory, horses, and fame anyone could possibly wish for.

THE TEN-MILLION-DOLLAR QUESTION

How much better to get wisdom than gold,
    to choose understanding rather than silver!
Blessed is the man who finds wisdom,
    the man who gains understanding,
for she is more profitable than silver
    and yields better returns than gold.
She is more precious than rubies;
    nothing you desire can compare with her.

                    —Proverbs 16:16; 3:13–15

IS GOD OBSOLETE?

Dear God,

I love you more than anybody else that I do not know.[1]

—WALT (AGE 10)

4

HIPPOS, SYRUP, AND SANTA CLAUS

A big white beard, a nose, and eyes, and a hat." Thinking hard, he added, "A white hat!"

It was one of those serious, uncle-to-nephew talks about God that seldom occur in one's lifetime. Swinging on a hanging wicker chair in my parents' living room was Josh, my cute, shoot-from-the-hip, four-year-old nephew. All of three feet and six inches, Josh was definitely in control—and he knew it.[2]

"Does the hat have any writing on it?" I asked.

"Nope," came his brisk reply.

Wanting to slip even further into his childish mind, I pressed: "What does God's hat look like?"

"It looks like Santa Claus's hat."

"Really? Where does God live?"

"Heaven."

"Do you know where that is?"

Prying his eyes from his stuffed monkey, he turned to me, "No. Do you?"

IS GOD OBSOLETE?

I couldn't fool this pint-sized genius. "No, I don't think anyone knows for sure."

"Maybe Nanny knows," he piped up.

Losing credibility fast, I moved on. "What does God do all day?"

"He lives in a house and has people over." Thinking a little more, Josh added, "He heals them."

He heals them; this was something essential I needed to take to heart in my medical career.

"And what does God make?" I inquired.

"He made me, and [pointing to the stereo] the speakers, [looking up] the roof, [glancing out the window] the trees."

I could tell his little mind was still spinning, so I asked, "Anything else God made?"

"He made the dogs ... hippopotamus ... skunk ... deer ... moose." Wracking his brain for a few more seconds, he couldn't come up with any more answers. "Ahh, that's it."

"Does God eat?" I asked, thinking it a reasonable question, considering we had just finished breakfast.

"Yep. God eats maple syrup ... pancakes ... bread ... and for lunch he has soup and ... bread." Stretching his little mind to the limit, he was at a loss again. "Ahh, that's it."

Then, before I could utter the first syllable of my next question, Josh grabbed his furry toy monkey, hopped off the swinging chair, and, as sincere as a four-year-old could be, said, "We'll talk again tomorrow, Uncle Bradley. Okay?" And with that, he dashed out of the living room.

Hippos, syrup, and Santa Claus; what did I expect, asking a four-year-old about God? Ask a child some difficult questions, and you are bound to get some mighty interesting answers! My conversation with Josh that April morning will remain memorable, not only for the humorous responses and our special uncle-nephew bonding time but also for the valuable insight I gleaned.

Puzzled, you might ask, "What amount of insight can you possibly gain from a monkey-toting four-year-old?" By the time you

reach the end of this book you'll know. And you may be surprised how it relates to you.

But if I surmised that I'd gleaned all the wisdom a child had to offer, I was dead wrong. A month later I found myself conversing knee-to-knee with the world's future theologians—a Sunday school classroom of seven- and eight-year-olds. *Surely if anyone could answer the tough questions,* I thought, *it would be this clever crew.*[3]

"Who is God?" I asked straight out.

Perched to my left on the edge of her seat was the radiant-eyed Nicole—the studious one. She didn't waste any time sharing her wealth of knowledge: "He's big!"

"Big! Bigger than this church!" burst out Amber, forgetting about her shyness. "Bigger than the whole world!"

Restless, yet seemingly focused on his Tonka truck, was Ira, an incredibly bright little guy with enough energy to power a small nuclear plant. "God is a perfect guy!" he blurted out (an honest answer for women who've wondered if such a guy exists).

Hoping to coax Ryan, Caleb, and Brooke into the discussion, I asked again, "Anyone else know who God is?" It was obvious that Ryan and Caleb, crouched at the head of the table, were the quiet ones—not really comfortable with the whole scenario. To my right was Brooke, bashful, yet attentive to everything going on, giggling from time to time.

"What does God look like?" I queried.

Nicole jumped back into the discussion, "You can't see him."

"No one can see him," added Ira, siding with his scholarly colleague.

"Does God sleep?"

"Yes," came Nicole's apt reply.

"When does he sleep?"

Giving it a little thought, she remarked, "Every seventh day."

(Every seventh day. Hmmm … reminded me of my surgery internship.)

"Does God eat anything?"

IS GOD OBSOLETE?

"NOOOOO!" echoed caroled Ira and Nicole on cue.

Okay.

As it was Mother's Day, I thought I'd toss out a related question: "Is God a woman?" I asked, a tad embarrassed.

"NOOOOO! He's a man!" they all chimed, laughing and giggling.

"Sorry." (How silly of me to ask such absurd questions.) Not wanting to insult their intelligence further, I delved into the meaty questions.

"What does God want us to do down here on earth?"

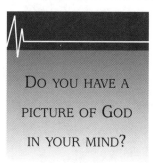

Do you have a picture of God in your mind?

Ira jumped to the challenge. "God wants us to teach people to believe in him more than the devil."

"Can we know everything about God?" I asked.

"No," retorted Ira.

"No one can," admitted Nicole.

"Well, how can we learn about God?"

Ira perked up, "By reading the Bible and going to Sunday school."

"Good answer, Ira. But does everyone believe in God?"

"Yep," replied Amber.

But Ira obviously didn't agree. "Not everyone believes," he insisted. "Satan doesn't believe, neither do bad people, Judas … the Pharisees … and the Romans."

The Romans; pictures of the magnificent Roman architecture popped into mind. So I asked, "Does God want us to be rich?"

"God wants us to give to the poor if we're rich," explained Ira.

Getting more answers than I bargained for, I pressed on. "You know, Nicole, there's probably another little girl named 'Nicole' in England, way across the ocean. Do you think God can hear both your prayers at the same time?"

She wrinkled her nose, "Gets kind of confusing for God to try and listen to two people at once."

(I've lain in bed wondering the same thing myself.)

HIPPOS, SYRUP, AND SANTA CLAUS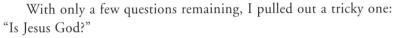

With only a few questions remaining, I pulled out a tricky one: "Is Jesus God?"

"No," said Ira—with reservation.

"Who was he then?"

"A guy who did miracles."

I didn't want to ignite a theological debate on the Trinity, but I thought I'd clarify the issue a little: "The Bible tells us that Jesus was God's Son, but that Jesus and God are the same. Many adults don't understand that."

Amber piped up, "Even kids don't."

With the session drawing to a close, I dropped my final question: "Why did God make the rainbow?"

Grinning, Ira couldn't help it. "To have a pot of gold at the end!" And with that he touched off a chorus of laughter around the room.

Five pipsqueak theologians, one medical doctor, and an honest discussion about God. It's a rather humbling experience when you realize just how much these little ones really know about their Creator. Even their Sunday school teacher, standing quietly off to the side, was amazed by their perceptive answers.

But I thought to myself, *Why stop here? Let's see what knowledge can be flushed out of the more experienced generation.*[4]

And so I took a little field trip to the local library to ask the cordial, laid-back librarian working there, "Who is God?" I had allowed her a week to mull over her answers to the three tough questions I had asked:

- Who is God?
- What does God look like?
- If you had the chance to ask God just one question, what would it be?

"God is bigger, more powerful, all seeing," she said, trying her best to define the infinite. "A huge presence … a lot bigger than Satan."

IS GOD OBSOLETE?

"Do you have a picture of God in your mind?"

"Not really," she replied. "I suppose if I ever thought of him as any shape, it would be a human outline."

"Do you think he has a body?"

She smiled and shook her head, "He's too big for all that."

When the third question rolled around, she admitted having conducted her own poll that week. "I asked this of other people," she confessed. "Most would ask God, 'Am I on the right track? Am I doing things the right way?'"

She seemed to be struggling with her own answer, so I tried to help, "Is that a question you might ask?"

Smiling again, she replied, "I like that one."

I thanked her, checked the religion section for any new books, and then returned home.

A few days later, I hopped back into the car and maneuvered down the chaotic Main Street, dodging pedestrians, bicycles, and unleashed dogs, arriving at a family-owned business. I had also allowed a businessman— a jovial, middle-aged chap—a few days to allow his answers to percolate.

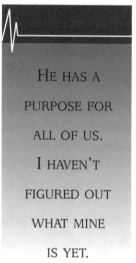

HE HAS A PURPOSE FOR ALL OF US. I HAVEN'T FIGURED OUT WHAT MINE IS YET.

"God is the Creator," he started off. "He created everything. God is the Most High, I'd say. Above him there is no other."

"What do you think God looks like?"

He chuckled for a few seconds before leaning forward on his sturdy wooden desk. "God said let's make man in our image. So I believe he looks like you and I do. He's got two arms, two legs, a head, feet, hands. That's what an image means—a reflection of, right?"

I was slightly confused, "Do you think God has a real body or a spirit body?"

"A spirit body, not a flesh body," he replied. "But it has a human form."

HIPPOS, SYRUP, AND SANTA CLAUS

A little more satisfied, I proceeded. "And what question would you ask of God?"

Mulling it over for a while, he finally settled on an answer: "What is his plan for my life? What is it that he wants me to do for him? He has a purpose for all of us." Then, chuckling again, he added, "I haven't figured out what mine is yet."

I thanked him, shook his hand, and promised to stay in touch.

I still needed more answers in my quiver, so I randomly selected a local video and DVD rental store. Strolling in, I spied a woman, probably late thirties, demure, working the cash register. After explaining my purpose and the triad of questions, she declined, confessing that she didn't have "anything to offer."

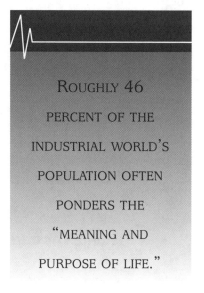

ROUGHLY 46 PERCENT OF THE INDUSTRIAL WORLD'S POPULATION OFTEN PONDERS THE "MEANING AND PURPOSE OF LIFE."

That was fine. I knew the questions weren't easy, and it was never my intention to force anyone to answer them. (I also knew at that moment why I hadn't pursued a career as a traveling salesman!)

After a few days of mulling over my next move, I decided to telephone my friend Dave,[5] a candid, sharp-witted surgeon I'd trained with some years back. Having never asked Dave these thought-provoking questions, I had no idea what I was in for.

We chatted for a bit before the question rolled around to, "Who is God?" I had offered Dave a few days to think over his answers, but he was more than happy to give his opinion on the spot: "God is what people who are needy in the soul believe in to make them more comfortable in life … a part of your personality not fulfilled. People go to church because they think God is there. If I were to believe in God, I wouldn't buy into organized religion."

IS GOD OBSOLETE?

I was somewhat taken aback, but at the same time, I had a good sense of where Dave was coming from.

We discussed the matter further before I asked, "What do you think God looks like?"

There was a brief pause on the line. "If there's such a thing [as God] it's a force of nature ... something like gravity. Not a person."

Unearthing some of Dave's rather uncomfortable memories, I discovered that he had grown up in a couple of different Protestant churches, eventually kissing the church good-bye at age fifteen.

"If there is a God, Dave, and you could ask him one question, what would it be?"

This time, the pause lengthened. "If there was a God," he replied, "I would ask 'Why is it that I don't have any faith?'"

Why do I not have any faith? A perfectly reasonable question considering that Dave had spent more than a decade in the church. After sincerely thanking him, I sadly hung up the phone, wondering just how the church could have disappointed my friend in his search for God.

PIECING TOGETHER OUR GOD MOSAICS

So far in my bold quest for knowledge of the Divine, I had picked the brains of a four-year-old, some seven- and eight-year-olds, and three adults. I found it intriguing that the majority of the grown-ups interviewed would ask God, "Am I on the right track?" Still, this shouldn't have surprised me, considering that roughly 46 percent of the industrial world's population often ponders the "meaning and purpose of life."[6]

But would I stop here? I thought, *Why not take a look back over the past three millennia at what some of the great leaders, writers, and celebrities had to say about God?*

And here is a sampling of what I found:

HIPPOS, SYRUP, AND SANTA CLAUS

THE REFLECTIVE:

God is a sea of infinite substance.[7]

—St. John of Damascus
Greek theologian and hymn writer (675–749)

The world is charged with the grandeur of God.

—Gerard Manley Hopkins
English poet and artist (1844–1889)

THE AMUSING:

Everybody's an artist. Everybody's God. It's just that they're inhibited.[8]

—Yoko Ono
US artist, musician (1933–)

God always helps madmen, lovers, and drunkards.

—Marguerite of Navarre
French poet and author (1492–1549)

THE CONFUSED:

God is the surprise of the universe, not its answer.[9]

—Dr. David Jenkins
Bishop of Durham (1925–)

God is Man & exists in us & we in him.

—William Blake
English poet and artist (1757–1827)

THE BIZARRE:

Not only is God dead, but just try to find a plumber on weekends.

—Woody Allen
Comedian, actor (1935–)

IS GOD OBSOLETE?

He was a wise man who invented God.

—Plato
(ca. 427–348 BC)

Plato is a bore.[10]

—Friedrich Nietzsche
German philosopher (1844–1900)

All of a sudden, the children's answers are sounding pretty good! It's easier to predict the weather than it is to predict what someone will say about God. People draw their knowledge of God from a diversity of sources to piece together their personal beliefs—or "God mosaics"—you might say. Popular resources include the Bible, church, television, movies, books, print media, radio, the Internet, and friends—along with another big resource we'll examine later. Just as no two people have the same fingerprints, likewise, no two people have exactly the same God mosaic—or understanding of God. No matter how many pieces line up the same, there will always be a slightly different configuration to each person's mosaic. Consequently, when we choose places of worship, we intuitively search for churches, temples, or synagogues where others possess a similar God mosaic.

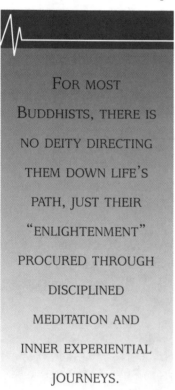

FOR MOST BUDDHISTS, THERE IS NO DEITY DIRECTING THEM DOWN LIFE'S PATH, JUST THEIR "ENLIGHTENMENT" PROCURED THROUGH DISCIPLINED MEDITATION AND INNER EXPERIENTIAL JOURNEYS.

In today's free-for-all faith-fest, challenging people to defend their faith has become politically incorrect—approaching downright rudeness, many would say. But let's imagine someone cornered you one day, challenging you to defend your understanding of God.

HIPPOS, SYRUP, AND SANTA CLAUS

Could you do it? Could you present a solid case for what you believe about God and why? Or would you shrink away in embarrassment with the comment, "We all have a right to our own opinion"?

Nicely ask someone on the street, "Who is God?" and he or she may fire back, "Who are you?" But chances are, you will receive honest, forthright answers, similar to the ones I received in my interviews—depending, that is, on where your street is located. To think that everyone cherishes the same God, or unnamed "intelligence," even in Europe or North America, would be ignorant and naive.

Maybe it's time we took a closer look into how other religions view God.

THE "GOD" NEXT DOOR

Take an afternoon stroll down Tokyo's ritzy Ginza strip (Japan's answer to New York's Fifth Avenue), and you'll find yourself in shopping heaven, rubbing elbows with the wealthy elite and wishing your credit cards weren't maxed out. Let's suppose we stopped a handsomely dressed Japanese businessman and asked him (in our best Japanese), "Who is God?" Chances are, he might say he practices Nichiren Shoshu Buddhism, one of the many forms of Buddhism scattered throughout the world. He'd patiently tell you that this "God" does not exist; he'd explain that every day he reverently kneels before his *gohonzon*, a black, wooden box, holding the Lotus Sutra scroll, from which he recites sacred passages. The gohonzon, he'd tell you, holds "universal forces" that will govern his life.[11]

Yet not all of the estimated 350 million Buddhists worldwide hold the same gohonzon—or the same convictions. Implore a businesswoman on the same street—or a female entrepreneur approximately 5,500 miles away on Beverly Hills' Rodeo Drive—and she might proclaim that Buddhist dogma is for the dogs. Being a member of a new generation of Buddhists, she might say, "Something so simple as making pancakes, meeting someone, or

IS GOD OBSOLETE?

talking on the phone can increase one's spirituality."[12] All those long-winded prayers and drudging chants aren't necessary for real growth.[13]

Or press a Buddhist monk in Thailand, and he may denounce the existence of God, while admitting his cultural superstitions: "I believe there are spirits."[14] Or question a "New Age" Buddhist in Japan, and he or she might say, "All people become Buddhas after death—'God' exists in everyone."[15] Or sit down and chat for a while with one of the more than a million North Americans practicing Buddhism (many also practicing Catholicism or Judaism), and you may hear that reincarnation stops when you stop creating "bad karma" or that "the only way to end the suffering is by forgetting [the imagined] God and being self-reliant."[16] Richard Gere, an award-winning actor, once said, "I know that the source of all the energy in the universe is the god Buddha and the face of the Source is the face of love."[17]

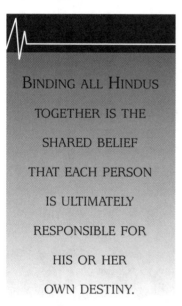

BINDING ALL HINDUS TOGETHER IS THE SHARED BELIEF THAT EACH PERSON IS ULTIMATELY RESPONSIBLE FOR HIS OR HER OWN DESTINY.

Founded in India around 525 BC, Buddhism is a world religion centered on the teachings of Buddha (Siddhartha Gautama). With many derivatives, including Theravada, Mahayana, and Zen Buddhism, no consensus seems to be found among Buddhists as to who—or what—they are praying to. (Buddha strictly forbade his followers to pray to him, but some do anyway.) For most Buddhists, there is no deity directing them down life's path, just their "enlightenment" procured through disciplined meditation and inner experiential journeys.

In contrast to Buddhism, Hinduism (with the exception of the Hare Krishna movement) has no particular founder, and most followers worship innumerable gods.

HIPPOS, SYRUP, AND SANTA CLAUS

Picture yourself hiking through the southern slopes of the Himalayas, enjoying spectacular views of the snowcapped mountain ranges above and the yawning river gorges below. All of a sudden, you find yourself eye-to-eye with a grinning, sinewy woman—an Indo-Aryan sheepherder—and knee-to-nose with her herd of sheep. Striking up a conversation with the cheerful lady, you discover that she is a Hindu, so you politely ask her, "Who is God?"

She'd probably smile and point, "See those mountains? Brahma, the Holy Creator, made every mountain. He created everything."

"So Brahma is God?" you ask.

"Yes. So is Vishnu the Preserver and Shiva the Destroyer. But my brother, a computer consultant in Washington, believes Shiva also creates and preserves."[18]

A little confused, you ask, "So you have more than one god, but you don't call him 'God'?"

"No, we have one God and Creator, Brahman." (*Brahman* is not to be confused with *Brahma.*)

"I thought you said *Brahma* was the creator and that you had other gods?"

Taking a stick, she draws a triangle in the dark soil. "Brahman is the eternal, impersonal, three-in-one God. He is the triangle, and everything inside it. Each triangle point represents a major personal god inside him: Brahma, Vishnu, and Shiva."

"So you have one god and three smaller gods inside him?"

She touches her stick to the triangle's center, "Inside the triangle are countless other lesser gods and goddesses, some of whom I also worship at the shrine in my home. All these gods and goddesses, and all life-forms, including the soul, are part of Brahman, the Divine."

After sipping tea around a small fire and sharing a tasty meal of buckwheat and sugarcane, you shake her hand and graciously thank the kind woman. Then you continue along on your hike, a little more knowledgeable of Hinduism and of the more than 760 million people on the earth who practice it.

Hinduism, one of the oldest religions, is also one of the most diverse in beliefs and practices. Some Hindus may worship one or more gods or goddesses, be theists or monists, or have a personal or nonpersonal relationship with the god(s) they bow to. But binding all Hindus together is the shared belief that each person is ultimately responsible for his or her own destiny. Equally binding is the belief that each religion's portrayal of God is in keeping mostly with the true character of the Hindu's god(s).[19] Of course, the reverse is not true: While people of most other religions consume millions of hamburgers each day, a Hindu will adamantly protest that, "The cow is a god incarnate."

With more than 1.5 million Hindus living in the United States, the drive to "maintain ethnic identity" has brought about the hurried construction of Hindu temples in hundreds of communities dotted across America.[20] But this impressive growth still pales in comparison to what is going on in America's Muslim community.

"The Hindu community is not anywhere near as well-organized as Muslims," reports Diana Eck, an expert on Hinduism and director at Harvard University's Pluralism Project.[21] Muslims, numbering more than six million in America, have surpassed the population of Jews, making Islam the second largest religion in the United States.

Picture yourself this time as an administrative assistant, shuffling between the twenty-fifth and twenty-sixth floors of a large skyscraper. One day thirst hijacks your tongue and you sneak into an infrequently used kitchen to make yourself a cup of coffee ... to find your coworker and buddy Carl, early thirties, standing barefoot on the marble tiles, his face, hands, and feet dripping wet.

You do a double take before ambling over to the coffeemaker. "What's the matter, Carl? They shut off the water in your apartment?"

"No," he laughs, grabbing more paper towels to wipe his feet. "I do this five times a day."

You grin back at him. "I know you're a clean freak and all, but—"

"It's for praying."

"What's for praying?"

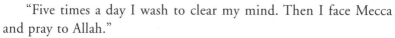

"Five times a day I wash to clear my mind. Then I face Mecca and pray to Allah."

"Allah?" You can't believe your ears. "Last month I saw you in church—"

Carl cuts you off abruptly. "I quit church. It just wasn't doing anything for me—you know what I mean? Now I attend a mosque, and I feel more connected, more spiritual."

"How can you quit church and just throw away God like that?"

Perturbed, Carl spins back to you. "I didn't throw away God!"

"Well, now you pray to Allah—"

"Allah is the Arabic name for God," he retorts. "All believing humans are Muslims in their hearts. 'As long as you don't reject the idea of a Supreme Being, then you are Muslim'" (an idea put forth by the Syrian Muslim thinker Mohammed Shahrur).[22]

You saunter past Carl to the sink. "I am *not* Muslim!"

"You are at heart, whether you admit it or not."

Now *you* are the one growing perturbed. "I worship the God of the Bible!"

"So do I!" exclaims Carl. "Allah is all-powerful, all-knowing, all-merciful, and the sovereign judge of the universe. I believe some of the Bible, but now I take my direction from the Koran, which Allah revealed to his greatest prophet, Muhammad."

You're not sure what to think at this point. Carl finishes tying his last shoelace and stands up. "Hey, I didn't mean to offend you or anything."

"N-no." Swiveling back to the sink, you run your own hands under the water. "No offense taken."

"See ya later!" And with that Carl turns and leaves the kitchen.

Choose a hundred people at random from our planet, and twenty of them will be Muslims. More than 1.2 billion Muslims are aggressively spreading Islam, making it the fastest-growing religion in the world. And though Allah may seem to be just a carbon copy of the Christian's God, many distinct and important differences should be pointed out.

IS GOD OBSOLETE?

A Muslim believes ...	A Christian believes ...
Allah is one in essence.	God the Father, God the Son, and God the Holy Spirit constitute the Trinity.
Assigning the name "Father" to Allah is blasphemous.	Calling out to him as "Father" pleases God.
Allah is too supreme and too far above humanity to be personally knowable.	God invites us to have a personal, intimate relationship with him.
Allah does not love sinners.	God loves sinners.
Allah offers no Savior.	God offers Jesus Christ as Savior to everyone.
The Koran calls Muslims to spread Islam and convert "infidels" with force and war.	The Bible commands Christians to spread the Gospel with love.
Allah guarantees paradise only to Muslims who die fighting a holy war; all other Muslims hope for the best, unsure of their eternal destination.	God guarantees salvation and eternal life in heaven with full assurance to all who call in saving faith on the name of Jesus.

Here is something, however, that the Holy Bible and the Koran can both agree on: Both teach that the Bible is God's Word. The Koran labels the Judeo-Christian Scriptures as "The Word of God," "The Book of God," and "a decision for all matters." Christians are encouraged to look to their holy Bible for God's guidance and revelation (Sura 5:50).[23] Of course, the Bible agrees fully with this teaching (2 Tim. 3:16–17). Even Muhammad (or his opponents— depending on your interpretation) is urged to test the accuracy of his teachings by comparing them to the divine teachings given in the Bible to Jews and Christians (Sura 10:94).[24]

HIPPOS, SYRUP, AND SANTA CLAUS

This is all very interesting because the teachings of Christ in the Holy Bible blatantly contradict the teachings in the Koran. Christ tells us that he is God (Matt. 26:63–67; John 8:58; 10:36; 17:5; cf. John 1:1–5). The Koran says that Christ is not God (Sura 4:171; 5:73, 74, 76; 9:30). Christ says, "I am the way and the truth and the life. No one comes to the Father except through me" (John 14:6). The Koran states that Christ was just another apostle of Allah (Sura 5:76).[26] He therefore is not the only way to paradise. Christ says that we can be guaranteed salvation by saving faith alone. Works are not needed for salvation (John 3:16; cf. Eph. 2:8–9). The Koran teaches that "deeds of righteousness" are in fact a requirement for *maybe* gaining entrance to paradise. (cf. Sura 4:57:5:10).[27]

WE NEED NO OTHER BOOK THAN THE BIBLE— NO FURTHER REVELATION FROM GOD TO LIVE LIFE TO ITS FULLEST.

Do you see the problem here? The Koran tells Christians to follow their Bible, "The Word of God," then it turns around and contradicts what God says.[28] Clearly, the Holy Bible and the Koran were not inspired by the same person. God tells us in the Holy Bible that his truth was "once for all" delivered (with no additions needed) to the saints by way of Christ's apostles (Jude v. 3). (Mohammed, Allah's apostle, was born approximately five hundred years *after* this verse was written.) In contrast to what Islam teaches, we need no other book than the Bible—no further revelation from God to live life to its fullest (Prov. 30:6; 2 Tim. 2:15; 3:16–17; Jude v. 3; Rev. 22:18–19).

As you can see, an immeasurable gulf separates the Bible from the Koran—and an immeasurable gulf separates God from Allah. Understandably then, Allah is not the one true God of Abraham, Isaac, and Jacob (see Gen. 15:6; John 14:6–7; Rom. 4:9, 13, 16; Gal. 3:8, 14; Heb. 11:9).[29]

IS GOD OBSOLETE?

Space does not permit a detailed examination of every religion. Neither does space allow for a critical analysis of all the "Hippos, Syrup, and Santa Claus" views of God. But with all these worldviews metamorphosing into a hodgepodge of pseudogods before our very eyes, it's important that we examine some startling trends. And where better to start than with the United States of America—the most religiously diverse country in the world?

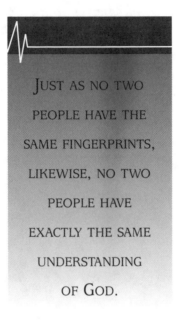

JUST AS NO TWO PEOPLE HAVE THE SAME FINGERPRINTS, LIKEWISE, NO TWO PEOPLE HAVE EXACTLY THE SAME UNDERSTANDING OF GOD.

IS GOD OBSOLETE?

While casual religious affiliation and activity gives people a sense of comfort and security, surprisingly few who consider themselves to be Christian center their lives on their faith. Most are neither satisfied with nor fulfilled by their faith experiences.[1]

—GEORGE BARNA AND GEORGE GALLUP JR.

5

HAS GOD BECOME OBSOLETE?

"I s God Dead?" taunted *Time* magazine on the cover of its April 1966 issue. About the same time, Emory theology professor Thomas Altizer and other like-minded theologians packed out lecture halls on some campuses by heralding the theory that "God died on the cross and never rose."[2] An unprecedented exodus from America's churches was fueling such conclusions,[3] and for a while, the church seemed rather complacent about the whole matter.

Six months later, the National Council of Churches took action. A strategic television ad campaign hit American homes with the countermessage "God Is Living."[4] It wasn't long before the citizens of America began trickling back into the church. Megachurches began sprouting up all over the nation, touching off a boom in church construction and renovations. Was this heightened religious fervor the result of the ad campaign? Or was this only the beginning of something else that would surface some twenty years later?

Despite the incredible jump in national church attendance, not every church denomination was enjoying standing-room-only services. In fact, over the next thirty years, the Episcopal and Presbyterian churches would watch their membership plummet by 20 to 40 percent, while the Mormon church (Church of Jesus Christ of Latter-Day Saints) "grew by 90 percent, Jehovah's Witnesses by 162 percent, and the Pentecostal Assemblies of God Church by 267 percent,"[5] making them the fastest growing denominations in America.

Had you asked Geoffrey Parrinder, a leading British theologian and expert in comparative religions, the reason for such failures and successes, he would have predicted back in the '60s, "Each faith's survival depends directly upon its ability to satisfy man's changing needs."[6] Looking beyond aggressive recruiting and marketing techniques, how did these three denominations succeed in gratifying their members' needs? As we're about to discover, the church wasn't the only party that clued in to America's "needs" and desires.

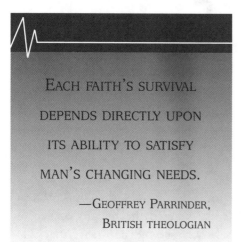

EACH FAITH'S SURVIVAL DEPENDS DIRECTLY UPON ITS ABILITY TO SATISFY MAN'S CHANGING NEEDS.

—GEOFFREY PARRINDER, BRITISH THEOLOGIAN

In the early 1990s, with church attendance still on the rise, an interesting phenomenon was taking place. Organized religion was gradually being replaced by something called "personal spirituality." Eugene Taylor wrote in *Psychology Today*, "We are witnessing a spiritual awakening unprecedented in modern times, according to scholars in American religious thought."[7]

By the late '90s, a record high 95 percent of Americans said they believed in God (or a higher power);[8] 89 percent believed that Jesus Christ was the Son of God; 84 percent believed Jesus Christ rose from the dead;[9] 66 percent professed a "personal commitment to Jesus Christ;"[10] and 60 percent conveyed that "religion is very important in their lives." Yet only 40 percent attended a religious service every week.[11]

HAS GOD BECOME OBSOLETE?

In a December 1998 *Dallas Morning News* article titled "It All Adds Up: Religion surveys find us more spiritual, less faithful," America's favorite religion pollsters, George Barna and George Gallup Jr., reported that 82 percent of Americans expressed the need "to experience spiritual growth," up an incredible 24 percent over the previous four years.[12] A "dramatic religious transformation," the greatest in the century, was quietly invading the United States, reported the *Los Angeles Times*, asserting that America was "fast becoming the most spiritually diverse country in the world."[13]

Then tragedy struck.

RIDING THE TIDAL WAVE

Did the terrorist attacks on September 11, 2001, add to this spiritual snowball effect? Interestingly enough, church attendance and interest in spiritual matters was already on a mini upsurge—even before the World Trade Center towers came crashing down.[14] George Gallup Jr.'s findings, presented the following January, surprised many—including himself:

> The initial analysis of the terrorist attacks' impact on the nation's spirituality shows that there has been no increase in church attendance or in the importance of religion in Americans' daily lives.[15]

Yes, Americans flooded their neighborhood churches for a few weeks, but it wasn't much different from the "holiday effect" seen at Christmas and Easter. The only element that changed was how Americans perceived the influence of religion. A whopping 71 percent said that "religion as a whole is increasing its influence on American life." Only 39 percent had said the same thing ten months earlier.[16]

A similar phenomenon presented itself in February 2004; only this time it was a movie—not a terrorist attack. The overwhelming success of Mel Gibson's controversial film *The Passion of the Christ* took Hollywood, and even the religious community, completely by surprise. In the beginning, many critics believed Gibson would never recoup the twenty-five to thirty million dollars he invested. The film has now turned into the highest-grossing R-rated film and the highest-grossing independent film of all time. In fact, 76 percent of American adults stated at the time that they had either seen or wanted to see Gibson's film.[17] From T-shirts to Jesus tattoos, from lapel pins to official "Jesus nails," Jesus Christ had easily become the year's hottest commodity in merchandising.

> PEOPLE TODAY ARE CERTAINLY HUNGRY FOR THE TRUTH; YET, AS SOME AUTHORS HAVE ALSO NOTED, MOST ARE UNWILLING TO COMMIT THEIR LIVES WHEN THEY EVENTUALLY FIND IT.

But did the movie truly change people's lives? Many said it did.[18] As after 9/11, some churches reported a rise in church attendance. Citizens were more open to talking about spiritual matters. Bookstores couldn't keep enough Jesus books on their shelves. Discussions about Jesus and God popped up everywhere, from radio shows to tattoo parlors. After watching the movie, some criminals were so consumed with guilt they actually turned themselves in. One Texas man confessed to detectives that he had strangled the mother of his child. She hadn't hanged herself as everyone believed.[19]

The movie definitely changed the weekly routine for many Americans, but did it result in the genuine conversions of millions? Christ had laid down his life for every moviegoer. Would every moviegoer now lay down his or her life for Christ? No doubt the movie left an indelible impression on the minds of many believers, and God probably used it indirectly to help bring about the genuine repentance and salvation of many. But for the most part, the film offered little more than a watercooler discussion piece for most nonbelievers. As one pastor remarked, *"The Passion of the Christ* does not answer the right questions, but it does raise them."[20]

Around the same time that Gibson's movie released, Dan Brown's famous book *The Da Vinci Code* sold more than six million copies. The best-selling fiction book, said to contain historical facts, stripped Christ of his divinity and declared that he had married Mary Magdalene. But this didn't seem to bother many—including millions of "believers." Jesus had become all the rage of 2004, and—God or not—people couldn't get enough of him. "Jesus Jams" and "Jesus Fests" and a whole lot of "spiritual shaking" was going on. But to many, Jesus was nothing more than a hip icon for a feel-good "spiritual" search prompted by a profound spiritual emptiness.

People today are certainly hungry for the truth; yet, as some authors have also noted, most are unwilling to commit their lives when they eventually find it.

LONE-RANGER SPIRITUALITY

I imagine even the cunning sleuth Sherlock Holmes would have difficulty piecing together all the poll data we've unearthed so far in this chapter. What's going on in America? Could the poll results following 9/11 and Mel Gibson's movie represent an even greater receptiveness to personal spirituality that is not, for some unknown reason, showing up in the statistical analysis on religion in America? Could this be the reason almost everyone is talking *about* Jesus, but few are actually living *for* Jesus? Are people, more than ever,

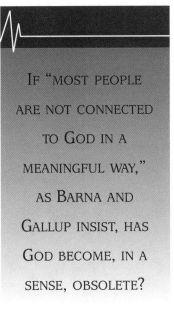

IF "MOST PEOPLE ARE NOT CONNECTED TO GOD IN A MEANINGFUL WAY," AS BARNA AND GALLUP INSIST, HAS GOD BECOME, IN A SENSE, OBSOLETE?

seeking after this trendy spirituality in an attempt to find meaning in life? Do they believe that true meaning can be achieved without true submission to the Son of God? Do Americans view personal spirituality differently than religiosity?

I believe, by and large, the answer to all these questions is yes.

Today America rides a tidal wave of spiritual revival, the likes of which was never seen in the previous century (a giant wave of water largely comprised of decades of unanswered questions about a God many now consider obsolete.) "Traditionalists worried the '60s might kill off God. Instead, the era seems to have uncorked a free-floating ether of spirituality," proclaims Hanna Rosin of the *Washington Post*.[21] But this spirituality phenomenon didn't begin with *The Passion of the Christ*. It wasn't jump-started by the terrorist attacks in 2001. It didn't begin in the church-attendance rise of the early '90s. It was "uncorked" as far back as the '60s. A record high 33 percent of American adults now claim to be "spiritual but not religious."[22] (Thirty-nine percent of American teens say the same thing.)[23] And these figures will only continue to rise.

What effect has this thirst for spirituality had in America? Listen to Barna and Gallup's findings:

> The perceived influence of Christianity and the acceptance of core Christian doctrines [have] all declined.
>
> Most people are not connected to God in a meaningful way. While casual religious affiliation and activity gives people a sense of comfort and security, surprisingly few who consider themselves to be Christian center their lives on their faith. Most are neither satisfied with nor fulfilled by their faith experiences.[24]

Does this push toward a self-absorbed spirituality, together with the pooh-poohing of church doctrine, translate into a pooh-poohing of God? If "most people are not connected to God in a meaningful way," as Barna and Gallup insist, has God become, in a sense, obsolete? Do we treat God like a bulky, obsolete cell phone that we just toss into the junk drawer, thinking possibly we might have some use for him in the future? Does this pervasive "God is obsolete" mind-set explain the gnawing dissatisfaction so rampant in religious circles today?

I believe it does. One father in Seattle related, "On Easter, my son and I go camping. You can't help but be spiritual out there."[25] Most individuals nowadays think they can achieve true happiness and real contentment by way of their "do-it-yourself spirituality." (Mark Galli, managing editor of *Christianity Today,* labels it "Lone-Ranger spirituality.")[26] Oh, they might consult God every once in a while to appease their consciences, but such individuals would choose to undergo painful root-canal treatment thirty times over—without anesthetic—rather than fully dedicate their lives to God.

"I CAN'T DO GOD"

Some of you who have been sheltered from this whole spirituality craze may be wondering just how someone can be spiritual without God. "I was disenchanted in Christianity," proclaimed a twenty-six-year-old Zen Buddhist from Minneapolis. "I felt there was a lack of spirituality in it. There was a lot of religion, but no actual spirituality."[27]

One *Showtime* episode of "Rude Awakening" (a rude adult comedy) featured a heroine addict trying to beat her addiction. Though the episode was fictional, the story hits close to home for many spiritual aspirants. The dialogue went something like this:

> IF THERE WERE EVER A TIME WHEN OUR HURTING, DISCONTENTED, AND MESSED-UP WORLD NEEDED AN UNDERSTANDING OF GOD, IT IS NOW.

> Heroine addict: "I need some spiritual guidance. My program says that I've got to embrace God, I've got to embrace

spirituality. But I don't want to do that. God is scary. God is a vengeful patriarch hurling lightning bolts. So I don't know what to do."

Friend: "Well, just think of angels, just think of John Travolta in 'Michael,' think about how he brought that sick puppy back to life. That's something that you can live with, can't you?"

Heroine addict: "Yes. Yes. OK. I can't do God, but angels, you know, that I can do."[28]

Why would anyone want to be spiritual without God? In the quest for spirituality, people are turning aside to angels, sacred goddesses, and extraterrestrial life forms—simply because they "can't do God." God's character just doesn't jive with their consciences. Like oil and water, God doesn't mix with their utopian sea of happiness. God is too scary, too unsettling for them to even think about. So if God doesn't mesh with my personal spirituality, then something has to go. Adios, God!

In essence, God is considered obsolete.

Sad, isn't it? If there were ever a time when our hurting, discontented, and messed-up world needed an understanding of God, it is now. Drug addiction, gang rapes, racism, "holy wars," child prostitution, school murders, random sniper shootings—and yet, ironically, God is thought of by many as a meddling killjoy without whom this world would be better off.

Before we go any further, maybe we should define exactly what this personal spirituality is that's taking the world by storm.

GOD DOESN'T
MIX WITH
SOME PEOPLE'S
UTOPIAN SEA
OF HAPPINESS.

IS GOD OBSOLETE?

We can be busy with religion, active in church work, but again, God does not come into it. We are thinking of ourselves from beginning to end. The whole world is doing this. Indeed, that is why the world is as it is—because it has forgotten God.[1]

—D. MARTIN LLOYD-JONES

6

THE GREAT SPIRITUAL SMORGASBORD

E ugene Taylor, in his well-written *Psychology Today* article "Desperately seeking spirituality," provides us with an insightful description of this phenomenon:

> [Spirituality's] motive power is not coming from mainstream institutionalized science, religion, or education. Rather, it is a popular phenomenon of epic proportions that is at once profoundly personal, experiential, and transcendent. The new awakening is directed toward an opening of the inward doors of perception and it is perceptually grounded in what the experiencer believes is a deeper level of the immediate reality than we normally have access to.[2]

Another definition in *American Demographics* nicely illustrates this trendy spirituality:

> [Spirituality] is the search for an experiential faith, a religion of the heart, not of the head. It's a religious expression that downplays doctrine and dogma, and revels

in direct experience of the divine—whether it's called the "holy spirit" or "cosmic consciousness" or the "true self." It is practical and personal, more about stress reduction than salvation, more therapeutic than theological. It's about feeling good, not being good. It's as much about the body as the soul.[3]

When individuals were asked to define "spirituality" for a Gallup survey,

Almost a third defined it without reference to God or a higher authority: "a calmness in my life," "something you really put your heart into," or "living the life you feel is pleasing."[4]

MANY ARE THROWING AWAY ORGANIZED RELIGION, CHOOSING INSTEAD THE MOST GRATIFYING BELIEFS AND PRACTICES FROM A SLEW OF RELIGIONS TO FORM A UNIQUE, THERAPEUTIC PERSONAL SPIRITUALITY.

It's not surprising, then, that most secular authors broaden the term *spirituality* to include an existential component. Millions of people around the world would say they are spiritual because they are on a "quest for meaning and purpose," which often includes a genuine interest in developing relationships with others, connecting to nature, cherishing values, living healthily, and reaching out beyond our material existence.[5] Again, there's nothing wrong per se with pursuing these things. It's just that this "therapeutic spirituality," with its illusion of "life purpose and satisfaction,"[6] quietly pushes God onto the sidelines and out of view. But as I've argued previously, true meaning in life can be obtained only by a right relationship with our

THE GREAT SPIRITUAL SMORGASBORD

Creator. Do a study sometime of the world's famous philosophical atheists, and you'll discover that the closer they inched toward death, the more hopeless, frightened, and miserable they became.[7]

What was their "life purpose and satisfaction" when they needed it most?

In this personal search for inner well-being and "direct experience" of the transcendent around the world, some surprising events are taking place. For example, "home altars"—personalized shrines to whatever being one worships—are becoming more and more popular, even in North America. Nancy Brady Cunningham, an expert on the subject, claims that the desire to design such a holy place of worship in the home (sometimes with candles, oil, fig-

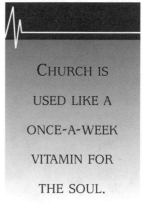

CHURCH IS USED LIKE A ONCE-A-WEEK VITAMIN FOR THE SOUL.

urines, and pictures of boyfriends and girlfriends) is similar to a fan's desire to plaster the walls with memorabilia and posters of a favorite sports or pop culture hero.[8] "I'm into spirituality, not religion" is a common catchphrase among spiritual aspirants and believers alike.[9]

It's no great shock, then, that church doctrine is rapidly being bulldozed aside by a "feel-good, do-what-I-want" spirituality that promises an inner utopian experience unlike anything else. Many are throwing away organized religion, choosing instead the most gratifying beliefs and practices from a slew of religions to form a unique, therapeutic personal spirituality. As one writer for *Life* magazine boasts, "I don't confine myself to the faith of my fathers anymore. All the religions are spread before me, a great spiritual smorgasbord, and I'll help myself, thank you."[10]

With religiosity on the outs, one might expect to see church attendance in freefall mode. It isn't. Yet church attendance hasn't kept pace with the rising US population. Over the last decade, the number of unchurched individuals has risen. When polled, 15 percent of respondents said they attended a church or synagogue about once a month, and 41 percent said they seldom or never attended a place of worship.[11] In 2002, the public's confidence in organized religion plummeted to 45 percent—the lowest figure since Gallup began polling Americans on the question in 1941.[12] (The number has since risen a little, to 53 percent.)[13] The reason the number of

TRUE SPIRITUALITY REFLECTS THE SOUL'S DAILY WALK WITH GOD.

unchurched is not significantly higher is this: Stepping through the doors of a church is generally considered therapeutic and stimulating for one's soul—especially when the whole family tags along. It might be the charming music, participation in the choir, the humor generated by the preacher who's funnier than Chris Rock, or just the whole social atmosphere under one roof. Church is used like a once-a-week vitamin for the soul: For the most part it's easy to swallow. It's cheap. It can't do any harm. And it makes you feel good when the preacher says the final "Amen"—like you've actually done your part to keep your soul in tip-top shape. And if you miss taking the "vitamin" in favor of exercising your muscles with some baseball or soccer, that's important, too, in the grand scheme of a healthy spiritual lifestyle.

And many churches are eager to do their part by turning this once a week "vitamin" tablet into an even easier-to-swallow smooth gel capsule. You can find a variety of self-help classes in many of the fastest-growing churches across America providing solutions to just about any problem in one's life, be it financial difficulties, marital problems, employment setbacks, obesity, or depression. There's nothing inherently wrong with these groups and workshops; it's just that attending church nowadays, for the most part, has little to do with one's earnest desire to draw into a meaningful relationship with God.

I often wonder if there would be a diminished need for these self-help classes in Christendom if we had a deep-rooted understanding of

God right from the beginning. If everyone had a better understanding of the holiness, sovereignty, and wisdom of our Creator and Lord, would we be suffering the psychological and physical fallout of extramarital sex, divorce, marital strife, deceit, pride, discontentment, greed, and pornography on our planet? Why do we place so little importance on learning about the character of God when we need it the most? Why don't we get to the root of our problems, rather than keep trying to slap Band-Aids on every ugly lesion that surfaces?

> We can be busy with religion, active in church work, but again, God does not come into it. We are thinking of ourselves from beginning to end. The whole world is doing this. Indeed, that is why the world is as it is—because it has forgotten God.[14]

Now don't get me wrong. Going to church and wanting to be spiritual is not innately wrong. I love meeting with fellow believers to worship and learn more about God. And I have to confess that I'm also into spirituality—not traditions and organized religion. But the apostle Paul wrote to the believers, warning them against setting their minds on ungodly things, for "to be spiritually minded is life and peace" (Rom. 8:6 KJV). The NIV makes it even clearer: "The mind of sinful man is death, but the mind *controlled by the Spirit* is life and peace."

THE REASON PERSONAL SPIRITUALITY IS A RUNAWAY HIT TODAY IS THAT IT IS ALL ABOUT "ME" AND VERY LITTLE ABOUT GOD.

What "Spirit" exactly is Paul referring to here? It certainly isn't a spirit of church tradition; it isn't this feel-good, remedial spirit so many are searching for today in the merry-go-round of personal spirituality, self-help workshops, Jesus nails, and tattoos. Instead, Paul encourages his fellow believers to strive after the Spirit of God, allowing him to control their minds, and ultimately their lives.

I ask Jesus' question again: "What good will it be for a man if he gains the whole world, yet forfeits his soul?" (Matt. 16:26a). "Life purpose" and "satisfaction," apart from God's purposes and blessings, are meaningless in the light of eternity.

Francis Schaeffer pinpoints for us what *true spirituality* is: "It is a continuing moment by moment proper relationship to the God who exists."[15] A proper relationship always involves two people—not the independent, overriding passions of one. True spirituality reflects the soul's daily walk with God—not the soul's daily run after worldly desires. The reason personal spirituality is a runaway hit today is that it is all about "me" and very little about God.

How many spiritual seekers can honestly say they are walking in harmony, step-by-step, with the Spirit of God? Millions around the world are excitedly strapping on their "spiritual parachutes" and jumping out of God's plane, hoping to splash into an inviting sea of health, success, and inner happiness. But where does this leave our Creator? It leaves God sitting at the controls of the plane, wondering if people have noticed that their parachutes are defective. Spirituality without the Divine is like a parachute pack with a missing or malfunctioning parachute. Sure, the jump is entertaining for a while—until one hits the ground, only to discover that spirituality without God is a desolate desert of nothingness, propagated by an individualism-obsessed culture and a don't-tell-me-what-to-do society.

The "great spiritual smorgasbord" has, ironically, left many a person completely famished.

A CUSTOMIZED CREATOR

This issue has two faces. On the flip side of the spirituality coin is a quest generation—people who genuinely seek God, placing much more emphasis on exciting experiences rather than boring and

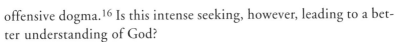

offensive dogma.[16] Is this intense seeking, however, leading to a better understanding of God?

I'll let you decide.

"In this new wave of religion," reports the *Tampa Tribune,* "people eschew traditions and adapt God to fit their needs." In reaching this conclusion, the newspaper interviewed Ed and Joanne, a couple living in Virginia. Fed up with the impracticalities of the Catholic school and church, the couple decided to:

> build their own church, salvaging bits of their old religion they liked and chucking the rest. The first [beliefs] to go were an angry, vengeful God and hell—"That's just something they say to scare you," Ed said.
>
> They kept Jesus, "because Jesus is big on love."[17]

In their search for God, the couple turned to newfound sources of wisdom in the local bookstore's Private Spirituality section, choosing such titles as *A Course in Miracles* and *Conversations with God.*

> Now they commune with a new God, a gentle twin of the one they grew up with. He is wise but soft-spoken, cheers them up when they're sad, laughs at their quirks. He is, most essentially, validating, like the greatest of friends.
>
> And best of all, he had been there all along. "We discovered the God within," said Joanne. "That's why we need God. Because we are God. God gives me the ability to create my own godliness."[18]

Ed and Joanne's quest to customize God into a practical and validating friend is a popular trend—but not with the Vatican. Pope John Paul II warned against this "cafeteria Catholicism"—picking what you want from the faith, leaving behind what you don't like—stating that it has resulted in a "crisis of meaning" in our world today.[19]

Paul Johnson, journalist, historian, and Catholic author of *The Quest for God,* asserts, "We are less sure about what God is, or what he means to us, than our parents were."[20] *Life* magazine reports, "*America's* God is vaguely defined,"[21] and the *Minneapolis Star Tribune* wonders if America's "much-touted religiosity is only 'skin-deep'" after Gallup dubbed America a "nation of biblical illiterates."[22] Earlier in the '90s, a Barna poll found that 82 percent of adult Americans believe "God helps those who help themselves,"[23] and "56 percent mistakenly think the idea comes directly from the Bible."[24] Later polls demonstrated that less than half of American adults can list the four gospels, and 70 percent of teenagers can't tell you why Christians celebrate Easter.[25] One in two Americans doesn't know that the first book in the Bible is Genesis. And 10 percent believe that Noah's wife was Joan of Arc.[26] No wonder Barna and Gallup concluded, "Most people are not connected to God in a meaningful way."[27] Never has America been so "spiritual," yet so ignorant of God and his Word.

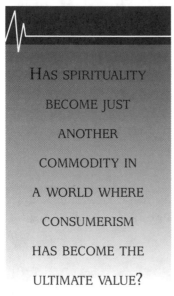

HAS SPIRITUALITY BECOME JUST ANOTHER COMMODITY IN A WORLD WHERE CONSUMERISM HAS BECOME THE ULTIMATE VALUE?

Cashing in on this spiritual hype is a multibillion-dollar industry, aggressively marketing personal spirituality to a world hungry for meaning in life. Innovative Hollywood-style videos, tapes, workshops, wellness treks, and weekend seminars have flooded America, promising everything from aura adjustments and communication with angels to a knowledge of mystical kabbalah, magic crystals, and transcendental meditation.[28] Such creative methods as Celtic Christianity, Christian mysticism, medieval chanting, liturgical dance, and guided meditations are advocated for those spiritual seekers "disenchanted" with the usual way of embracing Christ.[29]

This sought-after therapeutic revolution has resulted in spirituality becoming the fastest-growing sector in book publishing,[30] with sales totaling about one billion dollars a year.[31] A few clicks on the Internet and you can have FedEx deliver your spiritual how-to book, video, or tape to your door by 10:00 a.m. the next day—for a small fee, of course. "Is America experiencing a religious revival?" wrote one writer in *Newsday.* "Or has spirituality become just another commodity in a world where consumerism has become the ultimate value?"[32]

America may be the great trendsetter and marketing guru when it comes to personal spirituality, but don't fool yourself; the rest of the world isn't far behind. As we've already discovered, youthful generations of energetic Buddhists, Hindus, and Muslims everywhere are bucking religious traditions and doctrine, choosing instead a designer spirituality that not only looks good, but feels good.

Stephen Batchelor's book *Buddhism Without Beliefs,* for example, proposes tossing away "all that boring karma and reincarnation stuff."[33] William Boom, a London-based writer, sees the demise of "disciplinarian religions," citing Japan's new generation that resists being forced to "swallow ancestor worship!" Why squander my time worshipping some boring old spirit when I can attend all these energizing workshops and feast my mind on all these inspiring books?[34] Ronald F. Inglehart from the University of Michigan assures us that while "church attendance is declining in nearly all advanced industrial societies, spiritual concerns more broadly defined are not."[35]

Exemplifying this decline, attendance at mainstream churches in Australia fell by 10 percent over the '90s,[36] and a half-century falloff in Canada's church attendance has left only 26 percent of Canadians in a church pew on a weekly basis.[37] In Europe, church attendance has reached frightening lows, causing Europe's Roman Catholic bishops to declare, "There is a great risk of de-Christianization and paganization of the Continent."[38] While church attendance remains fairly high in Catholic hot spots such as Ireland and Italy, only 12 percent of British residents[39] and less than 10 percent of the youth in Belgium, Germany, and France regularly step through the doors of a church.[40] Some churches that once thrived in Western Europe now stand as laundromats, bars, discos, and warehouses.[41]

IS GOD OBSOLETE?

But many aren't worried. As one Dutch scholar put it, "Institutional religiosity is on the decline, but personal religiosity is not in danger."[42] In America they call the trend personal spirituality; in Europe they commonly label it "personal religiosity."

In the rest of the world, the statistics seem to tip the scales in the opposite direction. Researchers from the University of Michigan studied sixty-five societies and found that church attendance was rising in formerly Communist societies; however, in developing countries the results varied.[43] In contrast to North America and Europe, Christianity is spreading like wildfire across parts of Africa, Asia, and South America.[44, 45] However, with such a thirst for the supernatural in these mostly charismatic churches, new converts are fast becoming easy prey for this deceptive spirituality.[46, 47] It won't be long before Africa, Asia, and all the other continents jump on the spirituality bandwagon with America.

It's only a matter of time.

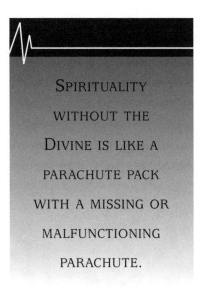

SPIRITUALITY WITHOUT THE DIVINE IS LIKE A PARACHUTE PACK WITH A MISSING OR MALFUNCTIONING PARACHUTE.

Part Two

AVOIDING THE PITFALLS

PUTTING THE PIECES TOGETHER

L ooking back over the previous chapters, we've chatted with a four-year-old, shared a table with a Sunday school classroom of seven- and eight-year-olds, discussed God with characters around the globe, and discovered this pervading and deceptive trend known as personal spirituality. It's time now to put all the pieces together: to use the insight we've gained (or are about to gain) to avoid some dangerous pitfalls that could prevent us from gaining a true understanding of God.

7
THE BIG PICTURE

What effect is this sham spirituality having on the world's understanding of God?

We've already read how one couple in America, Ed and Joanne, molded their God into an acceptable being by chucking parts of their Catholic teaching and keeping others. By the same token, millions are shunning the Bible, choosing instead to look inward for answers.

Take, for example, Denise, a woman from Georgia who wrote this curious letter to *Life* magazine:

> It amazes me that so many people are still lost as to what or who God is. The answer is within us all. That some choose to follow printed or spoken words on what they should do and feel about God is sad. People need to listen to their inner feelings because they tell what best defines God. My God is hopeful, supportive, humorous, joyful and never judgmental. My God would never punish any of us for a decision or choice we have made.[1]

IS GOD OBSOLETE?

"My God is my imagination." It may sound rather harsh, but that's really what Denise is saying.

What is indeed sad is that this philosophy reflects all too well the pervasive philosophy of today: the thinking that if we can just dig deep enough into our inner beings, into the subterranean recesses of our hearts and souls, somehow, we will be able to intuitively reason out who God really is—if we believe he even exists.

The great Arthur W. Pink, admired pastor in Great Britain, Australia, and America, declared that the god of the twentieth century had become "a figment of human imagination, an invention of maudlin sentimentality."[2] Pink used the analogy of an isolated tribesman who one day finds a glistening watch in the sand. The tribesman turns the watch over in his hands, carefully examining the gold casing, the mineral-glass crystal, and the highly polished watch face—trying his best to reason out the watchmaker who fashioned it.

But that's foolish, isn't it? For how can you reason out the complex character of the watchmaker by merely examining the watch? As Pink later asks, "Is the eternal and infinite God so much more within the grasp of human reason?"[3] Of course not. You can't accurately reason out the unique details of God's character by looking inside

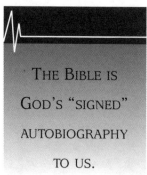

THE BIBLE IS GOD'S "SIGNED" AUTOBIOGRAPHY TO US.

yourself any more than you can reason out the unique details of the watchmaker's character by looking inside a watch. We could spend the rest of our lives viewing every nanometer of the watch with a high-powered microscope to conclude that the watchmaker is creative, ingenious, organized, and meticulous. But how can one determine if the watchmaker is left-handed, is moral, or loves justice, by examining only the watch? Likewise, how can we determine that God is transcendent, just, holy, wrathful, merciful, and completely sovereign by only studying creation? It's somewhat like trying to reason out a prospective mate's personality on an Internet dating service by viewing only his or her photo holding a birdhouse they just made by hand, but ignoring hundreds of pages they wrote in their profile.

God has certainly revealed himself to us in his wondrous creation, known as "general" or "natural revelation" (see Ps. 19:1). But no matter how much insight we glean about God from his creation, it still pales in comparison to the wealth of knowledge we can glean from the Holy Bible ("special" or "supernatural revelation"). While natural revelation is general, restricting us in our understanding of God, special revelation is miraculously definitive, revealing God's character to us in precise and intimate detail. The Bible is, in a sense then, God's "signed" autobiography to us.

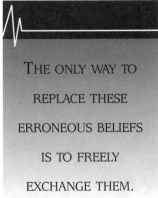

THE ONLY WAY TO REPLACE THESE ERRONEOUS BELIEFS IS TO FREELY EXCHANGE THEM.

Andrew M. Greeley, well-known priest, sociologist, and author of more than thirty best-selling novels, writes this in his autobiography, *Confessions of a Parish Priest:*

> The Catholic imagination is analogical: it sees God as similar to the people, objects, events and relationships of life. It would quickly add that God is different from all these, but Catholicism will still, in its first instincts, declare the similarity between God and world and only in its second instincts assert also a dissimilarity.[4]

Written in 1986, Greeley's words take on even greater significance today—and not just for the Catholic faith. In an attempt to reason out God, people claim to be looking inward for truth—while in fact, they are instinctively, and subconsciously, looking outward to everyday "people, objects, events and relationships of life" to piece together God.

When we set off to reason out God's character, we don't invent the raw data that feeds our cerebral reasoning machine. Like a modern factory, our brains have all the high-tech tools and machinery needed, ready at the push of a neuron to fly into production. But obviously you can't produce your God mosaic without the raw materials. How could you imagine in your mind what the colors orange or green look like if you had been born blind?

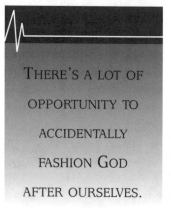

THERE'S A LOT OF OPPORTUNITY TO ACCIDENTALLY FASHION GOD AFTER OURSELVES.

Arriving in this world with our minds a blank slate, we instinctively look *outward* in search of likenesses and ideas to throw into our reasoning machine. By doing so, we are able to manufacture a decent product, filling in the holes of our knowledge base. It's too unsettling for us to travel through life with all these irksome potholes in our subconscious. Something has to fill in the gaps—and something usually does.

These "first instincts" referred to by Greeley are definitely the hardest to erase. Our ideas of God that we churn out from this instinctive outlook go on to pervade the depths of our subconscious, making these deeply ingrained beliefs extremely difficult to uproot. The only way to replace these erroneous beliefs is to freely exchange them with the real truth about God or, as often occurs, with something else that pacifies our logic equilibrium—even if that "something else" should happen to be false.

"There's a lot of opportunity to superimpose our view of ourselves on top of God, a lot of opportunity to accidentally fashion God after ourselves," write Michael Shevack and Jack Bemporad in their book, *Stupid Ways, Smart Ways to Think About God.*[5] Consequently, this process of intuitively reasoning out God should not be taken as a harsh criticism of any particular religion; rather, it should be viewed as a congenital weakness inherent in humanity.

Take for example this letter from seven-year-old Liz Marie:

Dear Lady God,

I love you. And I want to thank you for making the color pink. Pink is a beautiful creation.

I think in Heaven you must have made everything pink. Pink cushions, pink houses, even pink clouds.

I just hope the boys don't feel too out of place. That would be too bad.

I love you lots,
Marie (age 7)[6]

Little Liz Marie loved the color pink and intuitively concluded that God, like her, must also possess two X chromosomes and harbor an obsession for the color pink. Presumably, no one had explained to this child that God calls himself "Father" throughout his autobiography.

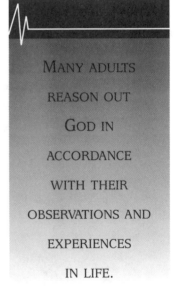

MANY ADULTS REASON OUT GOD IN ACCORDANCE WITH THEIR OBSERVATIONS AND EXPERIENCES IN LIFE.

This innate weakness also surfaced a few times in my conversation with four-year-old Josh. When I asked my little nephew, "What does God eat?" Josh, like Liz Marie, had no pop-up knowledge base to draw on. So how did he deduce the answer? Well, Josh's little brain probably put everything together something like this: "If I eat, God must also eat. And if I love to chow down on pancakes, syrup, and bread, then God must also love to chow down on the same foods."

Now contrast Josh's peculiar reasoning with that of the seven- and eight-year-olds. When I put the question, "Does God eat?" I received a resounding "NOOOO!" Over the previous three years, these little minds had been taught in Sunday school (and likely at home) that

IS GOD OBSOLETE?

God is our heavenly Father who does not need to eat, take a bath, or go to the bathroom. If these seven- and eight-year-olds had been given no knowledge base to draw from, they would have, like Josh and Liz Marie, looked *outward* for the answers. There are many seven- and eight-year-olds who still believe that God the Father eats. Even some older children do:

> Dear Father of the universe,
>> Since the whole galaxy is yours you must have a great family barbecue!
>
>> Invite me.
>> Chip (age 11)[7]

> SINCE MOST OF US VIEW LIFE FROM A HORIZONTAL PERSPECTIVE, OUR PRIORITIES AND NEEDS ARE FREQUENTLY DEFINED BY EARTHLY DESIRES—NOT HEAVENLY DESIRES.

Remember that when asked what God does in his spare time, Josh replied, "He lives in a house and has people over." Our families often invite guests, and Josh simply reasoned that our hospitable God must do likewise in his big house.

Like the ankle-biter generation, many adults reason out God in accordance with their observations and experiences in life. Like Denise, many gaze around at the splendor of this world and reason that a great God of love could never be judgmental and punish his children. How could a loving Father, responsible for such magnificent beauty and caring detail, send people to a fiery hell? Meanwhile others, grieved by all the tragedies around the globe, reason that a God of love either doesn't exist or isn't in control.

People will draw an unlimited number of far-reaching conclusions from looking outward. Richard Dawkins, promoted to professor of public understanding at Oxford University in the '90s, argued that the immense size of the universe was proof enough of God's nonexistence (a view also taken by H. G. Wells). In reasoning away God, Dawkins felt, "there was just too much for him to be supreme over."[8]

Interesting.

One Catholic priest bid *bon voyage* to his faith and the priesthood because he couldn't conceive of a God who would allow nuclear weapons to exist.[9] We all, to some extent, falsely draw conclusions about God based on the information our finite senses relay to us.

That being so, we still haven't satisfactorily answered the big question: What criteria do people use to form their personal God mosaic?

POKÉMON AND POKÉGODS

Listen to what Martha Fay, author of *Do Children Need Religion?*, says: "Kids given an unsatisfactory god by parents or Sunday school will invent a god they can live with."[10] Similarly, we "big kids," when given an inadequate and unacceptable god, will also "invent a god we can live with."

"Throughout history people have discarded a conception of God when it no longer works for them," writes Karen Armstrong.[11] My friend Dave openly shared that his Sunday school's portrayal of God "just didn't click." "If there's such a thing [as God] it's a force of nature ... something like gravity. Not a person," he said. (Seventy-seven percent of Canadians who believe in God consider him to be an "impersonal spiritual force." Only 17 percent of Canadian believers consider God to be "a person.")[12] Dave's response, like that of millions of others, is likely rooted in this subconscious thinking: If a personal God really exists who is sovereign, all-powerful, and all-knowing, then I would have to become accountable, change the way I live my life, and enter into a personal relationship with him. But that's not a God I can live with. So if I can relegate God to a mere force, something like gravity, then this is an acceptable God that can coexist with my personal beliefs—and stay out of my personal space.

For a *Life* magazine special feature, the authors interviewed fifty-six kids in six locales in America. Upon asking the kids, "Who is God?" or "What is God?" the investigators discovered that, regardless of the children's faith backgrounds, each child "depict[s] the god they need."[13] The "Dear Lady God" letter is proof of that.

This is the second criterion we use in piecing together our God mosaic: *the God we "need."* If you desperately need support and structure in your chaotic life, then you will mold God into an all-supporting Creator. If you were a member of the *Guinness Book of World Record's* most dysfunctional family growing up, then you will likely try to mold God into an all-loving, and all-accepting Parent (yet your relationship will be strained). If you declare bankruptcy more often than you renew your driver's license, then God will exist primarily as your "celestial loan officer." And if you're like an alligator in New York's vast network of underground sewers, floundering around in life's waste with absolutely no direction, then God will function as your obliging tour guide to the light at the end of the tunnel. But if you are incredibly successful, and feel you don't require God's expedient services, then you may never give God much thought—until, perhaps, disaster strikes.

> YOU WILL NEVER COME TO A TRUE UNDERSTANDING OF GOD UNTIL YOU FIRST STOP FASHIONING GOD INTO SOMETHING HE ISN'T.

Finishing out the twentieth century was the big Pokémon (short for pocket monsters) craze among kids, whereby kids would tote around flashy Pokémon cards in their pockets, trading them at will with friends and enemies. A similar craze can be found today in the grown-ups' world.

Digging through our society's dirty laundry, we discover that a chic "Poké-god" is gradually replacing the one true God of the Bible. We possess at best an impersonal, unpretentious, two-dimensional "Pokégod" (pocket god) that we shove into our pockets, making us feel all tingly and spiritual. From time to time we proudly slip out our prized cards to impress our

THIS GLOBAL SPIRITUALITY TREND HAS ALREADY SUCCEEDED IN DEMOTING GOD TO A ONE-DIMENSIONAL, NEAR-OBSOLETE BEING WHO EXISTS ONLY TO SATISFY OUR NEEDS WITHOUT GET-TING IN THE WAY OF OUR CONSCIENCES.

friends. Or, when the chips are down, we reach into our pockets, gaining reassurance that our treasured "Pokégod" is still with us. Or sometimes we see someone else's "Pokégod" we like better, and quickly trade ours away in an effort to "have it all." Many similarities exist between the "Pokés"; unlike the fleeting Pokémon fever, however, the great "Pokégod" craze is here to stay.

By instinctively looking outward, we reason out God's character along two criteria:

1. The God we can live with
2. The God we need

IS GOD OBSOLETE?

Now, you might think that the God we *really* need would automatically be the God we can live with, but such is not usually the case. Since most of us view life from a horizontal perspective, our priorities and needs are frequently defined by earthly desires—not heavenly desires. As a result, we often find ourselves plea-bargaining with God for bigger homes, newer cars, glamorous careers, and perfect health—to go along with the perfect mate. My friend Dave wasn't too far off the truth when he said, "[God is] what people who are needy in the soul believe in to make them more comfortable in life." Many needy people mold God into their "cosmic bellhop" whose sole purpose is to satisfy their every need and desire.[14]

Having said that, you don't have to be "needy" to mold God into someone he isn't. It makes little difference if you are the most famous agnostic in America, or the most famous evangelist in the world, if you try to reason out God's character in your mind without using the correct stepping-stones supplied in God's Word, you will invariably invent a false god you can live with—or an obsolete god you can live without.

Sadly, we often miss out on the God we *really* need: an altogether holy, just, righteous, loving, and wise God who offers us divine Grade A filet mignon in exchange for our dreary, daily regimen of $1.69 hamburgers; never-ending spiritual blessings in exchange for fleeting material thrills; imparted righteousness in exchange for do-it-yourself "salvation"; eternal life in exchange for a passing life of hedonism. Strangely enough, this is not a God many can live with.

Whatever your view of God may be, this you can be sure of: You will *never* come to a true understanding of our most awesome God until you first toss away these destructive criteria and stop fashioning God into something he isn't. God is not your loving tour guide, your "celestial loan officer," or your "cosmic bellhop," jumping up to serve you at your beckoning. Just as a watchmaker cannot be a slave to his ticking creation, God cannot be a slave to our demanding ID. Unfortunately, this global spirituality trend has already succeeded in demoting God to a one-dimensional, near-obsolete being who exists only to satisfy our needs without getting in the way of our consciences.

What is *your* view of God?

THE BIG PICTURE

The American psychologist Philip Rieff envisioned that "the new therapeutic culture would dilute religious faith into an amorphous, all-purpose 'spirituality.'" The astonishing part of Rieff's declaration was not so much *what* he said, but that he predicted this "all-purpose 'spirituality'" about forty years ago.[15] Although labeled "a most unfashionable sociologist in his time,"[16] Rieff does deserve credit for this insightful prophecy.

Or does he?

Almost two thousand years ago, while exiled on the small island of Patmos, the apostle John was forced to toil as a prisoner in the dark mines. Despite his arduous days and dismal surroundings, the apostle still managed to pen the book of Revelation under the inspiring hand of God. In it, John foresaw the day when there would exist a one-world economy, a one-world government, and a one-world religion (Rev. 13).

Of course, a hundred years ago people fell off their chairs laughing. How could all this happen? Russia, East Germany, and the United States of America under one monetary system? Britain and China worshipping the same entity? Every country under the leadership of one individual? It would be utterly impossible! Preposterous!

Today no one is laughing. We are edging closer to the realization of such epochal events as outlined in the book of Revelation. The onslaught of recent terrorist attacks is forcing the world to band together to fight back. Uniting is not wrong, but we have to admit that this unification will be a major catalyst for a new one-world order set up to police such international matters as money laundering, counterfeiting, human rights abuses, terrorist activities, and nuclear weapons disarmament and regulation. Eventually, "holy wars" will become so prevalent, and so hated, that the world will push to unite for a global religion.[17] And this trendy personal spirituality fits perfectly into the grand scheme of a one-world religion because it conveniently breaks down all religious barriers.

Hindus believe it doesn't matter which god(s) you worship, for it will be a Hindu god. A new generation of Buddhists, eager to banish all the rules, believes that a higher power exists in everyone.[18] Some Muslims are saying if you believe in a supreme being then you are Muslim at heart. And if this doesn't unite everyone, then "feelings" or experiences will. As one Protestant Christian put it, "The interest in spirituality is more related to experiencing feelings than engaging spiritual ideas. 'Spirituality' has the potential to be a natural integrator of life of all people everywhere."[19]

It doesn't really matter what you believe, or whom you believe in; everybody is worshipping the same god or force, with the ultimate goal of becoming more "spiritual"—developing or experiencing therapeutic "feelings" for the soul. No criticism. No right and wrong. No terrorist attacks. Just one big happy global spiritual bash with a welcoming invitation requiring only that you BYOS (bring your own spirituality). "Just as communism and capitalism will fade from our reality," says Sohail Inayatullah, chair of the School of Futures Studies in Queensland, Australia, "religion will as well, leading to some type of global spirituality."[20]

When the Antichrist, the man empowered by Satan to fight against God, finally arrives on the world stage, almost all people, no matter what religion or belief system they adhere to, will band together to worship the leader in their unique "spiritual" ways.

It won't be long now.

SADLY, WE OFTEN MISS OUT ON THE GOD WE REALLY NEED.

IS GOD OBSOLETE?

SOLOMON'S CLUE #1

Celebrate for now, but savor one thing,
That which you have won, you won't need to bring,
For it can't be sold, lost, traded, nor bought,
It can't be taken, though many have fought,
So trade that mask for true comprehending,
Clean out the cobwebs, shed aura and wing,
'Cause there's just one map to the treasure sought,
Choose the wrong map, friend, and suffer your lot.

8
SOLOMON'S CLUES

I f Solomon were still around today, what "clues" would he offer us in our search for a true understanding of God? (These are the helpful fictional clues based on biblical principles passed along to us in the bizarre game show near the beginning of the book.)

Gaining a proper understanding of God demands that we recognize where it differs from this insidious trend known as personal spirituality.

First, you can't buy or sell true insight into God. You can't attend a weekend seminar for six hundred dollars or buy a how-to book to instantly catapult your "understanding" to higher levels. Sure, you can gain a knowledge of God in this book—the pieces to the puzzle— and I can pass along clues that will help you to organize the pieces and appreciate how one piece relates to another. But ultimately it is you, the reader, who must get down on your knees to fit together the puzzle pieces yourself, thereby forming a picture of God in your own heart. For it is you, and you alone, who must choose which path you will take on this quest.

Second, you can't easily trade or lose a true understanding of God—unlike people who switch religions or spirituality. You wouldn't say to your four-year-old son, "Jeffrey, I realize you don't know how to ride a bicycle, so here's what I'm going to do. I'll trade my understanding and skills in riding a bike for your ignorance. Okay? Good, now hop on the bike and start peddling."

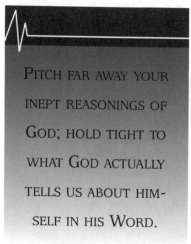

PITCH FAR AWAY YOUR INEPT REASONINGS OF GOD; HOLD TIGHT TO WHAT GOD ACTUALLY TELLS US ABOUT HIMSELF IN HIS WORD.

Third, an understanding of God can't be taken from us. Nero, Hitler, and countless others have fought in vain to wipe the belief in God off the planet. Millions have been tortured, imprisoned, beheaded, and tossed to the lions—yet nothing will shake a genuine understanding of God in the heart of a true believer.

What exactly did Solomon mean when he said, "So trade that mask for true comprehending."

If we were to pry apart the term *personal spirituality*, we'd find that the word *personal* is derived from the Latin word for "mask."[1] These trendy religious masks, representing this highly sought-after personal spirituality taking our world by storm, may look cool and may be the hottest selling items on the market—but if you look really closely you'll notice that they have no slits for the eyes. People everywhere are pulling on their "spiritual masks," fooling themselves into thinking they are truly spiritual when in fact they are blindly stumbling through life in search of the right path that will somehow lead them to the supreme being.

Ever try searching for someone while blindfolded? Ironically, many are doing just that.

In the last half of Solomon's clue, he advises us to "Clean out the cobwebs, discard aura and wing." Before we proceed on our journey, we must first do a thorough housecleaning of our cluttered minds to get rid of all the dust mites, garage-sale junk, and cobwebs (our previously imagined concepts of God) so that we'll have room for the *real treasure*. As difficult as it may be, I sincerely urge you to toss away all those not-so-true concepts and imaginary ideas that have piggybacked their way through your mind's door on the backs of humanistic reasoning and feelings (auras). Don't litter your mind with the spiritual worship of goddesses, mother earth, or angels (wings). Instead, carefully analyze your beliefs of God: Are they solidly based on truth? Or are they founded instead on hippos, syrup, and Santa Claus? Are you ready, with every fiber of your being, to seek after the one true God of the universe whom you *need?* Or have you consigned yourself to living with a one-dimensional, near obsolete god that you *want?*

The last line in the clue reads, "'Cause there's just one map to the treasure sought, choose the wrong map, friend, and suffer your lot." The path to intimacy with God is detailed in only one map. Almost all of us have ready access to this map, the Holy Bible, yet sadly some will grab hold of a fake map in our race for personal spirituality.

So I sincerely encourage you not to get caught up in this counterfeit spirituality hype that is overtaking the world. Don't look inward or outward for the answers to God—but instead, look upward. Pitch far away your inept reasonings of God; hold tight to what God actually tells us about himself in his Word. Resist the pressure to mold God into a flat, one-dimensional being; rather, behold God as our supreme heavenly Father who has multiple dimensions of infinite size. Don't empty your wallets on such distracting novelties as spiritual wellness treks, angel seminars, and healing crystals videos; instead, empty your heart of all preconceived imaginary ideas of God to make room for a true understanding of the Almighty.

You won't be disappointed, I assure you.

SCENES FROM THE JOURNEY AHEAD

A s mentioned earlier, the purpose of this book series is to guide a new generation of Christians along on a life-changing journey to intimacy with the Divine—a twenty-first-century-tailored quest that will increase the reader's understanding of the Almighty and radically impact the believer's life.

In the other books in the series, we will tackle some of the toughest questions ever asked of the Almighty. An MD Examines is a book series that one could pass along to a nonbeliever or to someone in the hostile trenches of everyday life. This series meets readers head-on in the problems and questions they are personally battling today.

Here's a sneak peek at some scenes from the other books:

WHY DOESN'T GOD STOP EVIL?

How often do we look out with dismay at the mess in our world and ask, "What was God thinking?" If there really is a good God up above, why is there so much evil in this world? If God is all-powerful, why didn't he bind up or destroy the Devil right from the beginning? If heaven is so great, why didn't God send us straight to paradise and forget earth all together? Where was God on September 11? And where was God when Hurricane Katrina struck? These and many other difficult questions are tackled head-on, providing fresh insight into some of the toughest questions ever asked of the Almighty. When the subject of evil is closely examined, we discover that there is a strong vein of wisdom and compassion in God's justice that Christendom has failed to recognize.

DOES GOD STILL DO MIRACLES?

Much debate lingers over the hot questions: Is God still performing miracles of healing today? If so, how common are they? Many Christian physicians, including me, believe God still performs miracles of physical healing that defy natural explanation. But are the hosts of "miracles" we hear about so often truly miracles? If these faith healings are not true miracles, then how does one explain the thousands of people who are instantaneously getting better? If the diseases being "cured" are not "all in one's head," then what biological mechanisms could possibly explain this phenomenon we're seeing? Why not just give God the benefit of the doubt and label every astonishing healing a miracle? What insights does God provide us in his Word? This book takes seriously Paul's mandate to "examine everything carefully" (1 Thess. 5:21 NASB). Some of the most fascinating and up-to-date medical and investigative research is examined in an attempt to uncover the truth about what is going on in faith-healing services and healing shrines around the world. A new generation of believers wants answers—and *Does God Still Do Miracles?* delivers.

SCENES FROM THE JOURNEY AHEAD

WHY DOES GOD ALLOW SUFFERING?

In this book we'll use the insight and understanding gained from other books in the series to help us answer one of the toughest questions ever asked of the Almighty: How can a God of love allow his children to suffer? Several inspiring true stories are presented, including the stirring account of how Steven Curtis Chapman faced the "thunder and lightning" in his life. This book goes further than most books on suffering by using illustrations and analogies to help the reader better understand the root cause of why we suffer. It also contains a unique story that helps us understand the real question at the heart of the matter: How can God be altogether just, kind, holy, righteous, and loving in the midst of our suffering? (See Jer. 9:24.)

At the end of each book we'll continue to examine a part of Solomon's fictional clues for some vital and practical insight into our Creator. By doing so, we'll break past the conflict barrier to illustrate the five levels of intimacy with our heavenly Father. And as always, we won't give up no matter how treacherous the waters, how yawning the valleys, or how lofty the mountains. An understanding of God will radically affect our lives like nothing else!

READERS' GUIDE
FOR PERSONAL REFLECTION OR GROUP DISCUSSION

Readers' Guide

Chapter 1
"May I Take Your Order?"

1. Why do people give up on God? Have you ever felt like chucking "the whole God thing"? If so, what were the circumstances?

2. In his experience as a doctor the author has observed that many people claiming to have a deep religious faith react just as much in anger toward God when tragedy strikes as nonbelievers do. Why is this? What is the difference between them and other believers who are able to experience tragedy without getting angry at God? Toward whom or what is their anger directed?

IS GOD OBSOLETE?

3. The author promises to "take readers' orders" regarding their most difficult questions about God. What is his purpose in doing this? What kind of God does he say he'll "serve up"? How does he plan to go about this? Do you think he'll be able to accomplish his goal?

Chapter 2
Make a Wish!

1. What's the difference between knowledge about God and a deep understanding of God? What importance does this difference have for us? How do we gain a deep understanding of God?

2. Are exhibiting happiness and contentedness the same as actually possessing inner peace and joy? If not, how do they differ? Where do true inner peace and joy come from?

3. How would you characterize your relationship to God—as a collection of facts about God, or as truly understanding him? What does the author mean by the term *God mosaic?* How do we go about arranging the pieces of our mosaic to gain a proper understanding of God?

4. How do we get a radically changed life?

CHAPTER 3
THE TEN-MILLION-DOLLAR QUESTION

1. What is the ten-million-dollar question? What is the correct answer to it?

2. Do you know people who would answer in the various ways the game-show contestants did? What would you say to them in response to their opinions?

3. If God visited you one night and granted you one wish, what would you wish for? What did Solomon wish for?

4. How is the divine treasure hunt like other treasure hunts? How is it different?

CHAPTER 4
HIPPOS, SYRUP, AND SANTA CLAUS

1. What do you think of the author's method of investigating what people think about who God is? What is his point in conducting this informal survey?

2. Who do you think had the best answer to the question, "Who is God?" Who had the worst answer? How would you answer that question? Does it make any difference how one answers that question, or is every opinion about who God is equally valid?

3. What do you think about the question Dave would ask God—if, as he said, there really was a God? Have you ever been disappointed by the way a church (or churches) you've attended has guided you in your search for God?

4. If someone cornered you, would you be able to present a solid case for what you believe about God and why? Do you find it easy to share your understanding about God with friends, or is it rather difficult?

5. What do you make of the pictures of God other religions have? How are they different? How are they the same? Which religion do you think is closest to Christianity?

CHAPTER 5
HAS GOD BECOME OBSOLETE?

1. What do you make of Geoffrey Parrinder's idea that "each faith's survival depends directly upon its ability to satisfy man's changing needs"? What's right about this statement? What's wrong with it?

2. There seems to have been a shift in understanding in the West away from traditional understandings about God and toward a self-absorbed spirituality that may or may not have anything to do with God. Have you noticed this shift among your friends? What do you think accounts for it?

3. Why would anyone want to be spiritual without God? Does this even make sense?

READERS' GUIDE

CHAPTER 6
THE GREAT SPIRITUAL SMORGASBORD

1. How does the publication *American Demographics* define spirituality? What, according to this source, are some of the characteristics of the new spirituality? Do you think there has to be a split between the head and the heart, between dogma and experience, when it comes to spirituality?

2. Does this new spirituality provide a way to understand the true meaning of life? Why or why not? What does a "godless spirituality" lead to?

3. The author quotes from a writer in *Life* magazine: "I don't confine myself to the faith of my fathers anymore. All the religions are spread before me, a great spiritual smorgasbord, and I'll help myself, thank you." Do you think it works to pick and choose from a variety of religious beliefs to construct your own personalized spirituality? Have you noticed this trend creeping into the Christian church? How has it manifested itself?

4. Why is personal spirituality such a big hit today? What is the ironic result of "the great spiritual smorgasbord"? What do you think about the trend to create God in our own image? Does this work? Why or why not?

CHAPTER 7
THE BIG PICTURE

1. According to Denise, a woman who wrote to *Life* magazine, where do people need to look to tell them what best defines God? What do you think of her idea? Is it a reliable way to find out about God? Why or why not?

2. What process does the author call "a congenital weakness inherent to humanity"? What are the dangers of creating our God mosaic by using this process?

3. Philip Rieff, a prominent psychologist, stated that "the new therapeutic culture would dilute religious faith into an amorphous, all-purpose 'spirituality.'" What is so remarkable about this statement? Do you think it has come true or not?

CHAPTER 8
SOLOMON'S CLUES

1. What are Solomon's clues?

2. What is the one map that will enable us to proceed on the path to intimacy with God?

3. What pitfalls should we avoid in our search for intimacy with God? What positive principles can we employ?

Notes

Introduction
Setting Our Sights

1. Casale Media, http://creative-quotations.com/one/694a.htm (accessed Jan. 5, 2006). This is a modern-day translation of the Latin text of Kempis's book, *The Imitation of Christ*, book 3 chapter 3.
2. If you are looking for a philosophic treatise surrounding the existence of God I would strongly encourage you to read Norman L. Geisler and Paul D. Feinberg, *Introduction to Philosophy: A Christian Perspective* (Grand Rapids, MI: Baker Book House, 1980).

Chapter 1
"May I Take Your Order?"

1. Jack Miles, *God: A Biography* (New York: Alfred A. Knopf, 1995), 232.

2. George Gallup, Jr., "Gallup index of leading religious indicators," *The Gallup Poll Tuesday Briefing*, (Feb. 12, 2002), www.gallup.com. See also Linda Lyons, "Age, Religiosity, and Rural America," *The Gallup Poll Tuesday Briefing*, March 11, 2003, www.gallup.com.
3. Gallup poll, quoted in Charles Austin, "Easter's Perennial Message of Faith, Hope, and Comfort," *The Record*, April 23, 2000, a01.
4. George Gallup Jr., "Poll Analyses: Americans More Religious Now Than Ten Years Ago, but Less So Than in 1950's and 1960's," Gallup News Service, March 29, 2001, www.gallup.com.
5. Philip Yancey writes, "Those who commit their lives to God, no matter what, instinctively expect something in return [from God]." I believe (as I'm sure Philip Yancey does) that it's more than just the committed who expect something from God.

Philip Yancey, *Disappointment with God* (Grand Rapids, MI: Zondervan, 1988), 37.

6. *The Columbia Encyclopedia,* Fifth Edition (New York: Columbia University Press, 1993).

7. The Agnostic Church, "Why Agnostics Can Believe in God," http://www.agnostic.org/BIBLE C-09.htm#P417_109441. The Web site points out, "The unknown nature of God includes any specification of whether God is singular or plural, and thus agnostics may not truly be classified as either monotheistic (singular God) or polytheistic (multiple Gods)," (accessed August 29, 2004).

8. J. I. Packer, *Knowing God* (Downers Grove, IL: InterVarsity Press, 1973), 14–15.

9. J. B. Phillips, *God Our Contemporary* (New York: The Macmillan Company, 1960), 9.

10. J. D. Douglas, Philip Wesley Comfort, and Donald Mitchell. *Who's Who in Christian History.* Illustrated lining papers (Wheaton, IL.: Tyndale House, 1997), Logos e-book.

11. Gerard Reed, *C. S. Lewis and the Bright Shadow of Holiness* (Kansas City, MO: Beacon Hill Press, 1999), 9.

12. Billy Graham, quoted in "Featured Author: Josh McDowell," http://www.leftbehind.com/channelinteract.asp?pageid=498&channelID=79 (accessed August 29, 2004).

13. Phillips, *God Our Contemporary,* 10.

CHAPTER 2
MAKE A WISH!

1. A. W. Tozer, *The Knowledge of the Holy* (New York: Harper & Row, 1961), 35.

2. George Barna and George Gallup Jr., "It all adds up: Religion surveys find us more spiritual, less faithful," *The Dallas Morning News,* Dec. 26, 1998, 1G. (Admittedly, those who call themselves born again or those who are labeled born again may not really be born again.)

3. Ravi Zacharias, *Jesus Among Other Gods* (Nashville: Word, 2000), 13.

4. Robert P. Lightner, *The God of the Bible* (Grand Rapids, MI: Baker Book House, 1978), 9.

5. John Calvin, *The Knowledge of God the Creator: Book One of the Institutes of the Christian Religion,* trans. Henry Beveridge (Grand Rapids, MI: Douma Publications, n.d.), 38.

6. Augustine, *Confessions,* ed. Henry Chadwick (New York: Oxford University Press, 1998).

7. Calvin, *The Knowledge of God the Creator.*

8. Lightner, *The God of the Bible,* 9.

9. Tozer, *The Knowledge of the Holy,* 9.

10. Ralph Waldo Emerson, quoted in Michael Horton, "The Agony of Deceit," *The Agony of Deceit,* ed. Michael Horton (Chicago: Moody Press, 1990), 23.

11. "Knowledge," *Similes Dictionary* (July 1, 1988), [Online] Electric Library Canada.

12. Dr. Joe Mikhael, MD, tape, (L'Amable, Ontario, Canada: L'Amable Bible Chapel, Nov. 4, 2001).

CHAPTER 3
THE TEN-MILLION-DOLLAR QUESTION

1. William Hamilton paraphrased by Charles Hodge, *Systematic Theology*, Vol. 1 (Grand Rapids, MI: Wm. B. Eerdmans, reprinted 1977), 351.
2. William Hamilton quoted in Hodge, *Systematic Theology*, Vol. 1, 351.
3. "'But let him who boasts boast about this: that he understands and knows me, that I am the Lord, who exercises kindness, justice and righteousness on earth, for in these I delight,' declares the Lord" (Jer. 9:24). The word *understands(eth, ing)* in Jeremiah 9:24 is used in the following nine translations: the KJV, NIV, NASB, NRSV, AMP (Amplified version), NCV (New Century Version), NLT (New Living Translation), YLT (Young's Literal Translation), and the Darby Bible. This word comes from the Hebrew word *sakal*, (stem = *hiphil*) meaning "to have insight," "ponder," "have comprehension," "act wisely," (*Enhanced Strong's Lexicon*, Oak Harbor, WA: Logos Research Systems, Inc., 1995), Logos e-book. In examining other verses in the Bible where the Hebrew word *sakal* is used, it would

appear that this understanding leans more toward an intellectual knowledge (or insight) than it does toward an understanding that fully comprehends, or discerns something or someone (cf. 1 Chron. 28:19). Differing somewhat from the Hebrew word *sakal*, the Hebrew word *biyn* means to discern, understand, be intelligent, know (with the mind) according to *Strong's*. The term *biyn* leans toward an understanding that discerns more deeply the intricate nature of something or someone (see Prov. 28:5). With the possible exception of Isaiah 43:10, this Hebrew word *biyn* is never used in regard to an actual complete understanding of God's true essence. (Note: the Hebrew word *biynah* (from *biyn*) is translated "understanding" in Proverbs 9:10b: "Knowledge of the Holy One is understanding [or discernment—*Strong's*].") The word *knowledge* in Proverbs 9:10 and the word *knows* in Jeremiah 9:24 are both ultimately derived from the same Hebrew word *yada*, which confers a close relationship such as that of an intimate relationship between a husband and wife. Paul tells us that we cannot completely know or understand God (1 Cor. 2:11; 13:12), but that we can clearly and plainly know God (Gal. 4:9). While the combination of an intimate relationship and a limited mortal understanding of our heavenly Father supersedes a simple intellectual knowledge, it does fall far short of attaining a complete understanding of God's true essence. Hence, we can understand God somewhat.

CHAPTER 4
HIPPOS, SYRUP, AND SANTA CLAUS

1. David Heller, *Talking to Your Child About God* (New York: Bantam Books, 1988), 68.
2. Interview conducted, Bancroft, Ontario, Canada, April 1, 2000.
3. Interview conducted, L'Amable, Ontario, Canada, May 2000.
4. Adult interviews conducted, Bancroft, Ontario, Canada, May–June 2000.
5. The name has been changed.
6. University of Michigan study cited in "Religious Service Attendance Dropping," United Press International (Jan. 15, 2000).
7. St. John of Damascus's birth date and lifespan are reported differently, depending on the source.
8. Yoko Ono in interview with Abram Deswaan for Dutch TV, Oct 1968, quoted in *Creative Quotations for Creative Thinking,* http://creativequotations.com/one/1200.htm (accessed March 5, 2003).
9. Connie Robertson, ed., *The Wordsworth Dictionary of Quotations* (Ware, Hertfordshire: Wordsworth Editions Ltd., 1996), 225.
10. These are actual quotes from Plato and Nietzsche put together in sequence by Byrne for comical effect, in Robert Byrne, ed., *1,911 Best Things Anybody Ever Said* (New York: Ballantine Books, 1988), 6; orig. pub. as *The 637 Best Things Anybody Ever Said, The Other 637 Best Things Anybody Ever Said,* and *The Third and Possibly the Best 637 Best Things Anybody Ever Said* (Three Volumes, 1982–1986).
11. Josh McDowell, *The Best of Josh McDowell: A Ready Defense,* Bill Wilson, compiler (Nashville: Thomas Nelson, 1993), 280–81; orig. pub. (San Bernardino, CA: Here's Life Publishers, 1990).
12. Khalil Abdullah, "Karma Thegsum Choling Dallas," *The Dallas Morning News,* Nov. 16, 1996, 2G.
13. Ibid.
14. Ben Barber, "Merit and Magic: Buddhism Faces Modernity in Thailand," *The World & I,* Vol. 13 (April 1, 1998), 216.
15. Nicole Gaouette, "Japan's Search for Spirituality," *The Christian Science Monitor,* Oct. 8, 1998, Features section.
16. Suwanda Sugunasiri, "Buddhists Keep Faith In Many Cultures," *The Toronto Star,* April 25, 1998.
17. Richard Gere quoted in David Ragan, "Some stars believe in God (and some don't)," *Cosmopolitan,* Nov. 1, 1995, 252–56.
18. According to the following article, Siva is the "Creator, Preserver and Destroyer of all existence." "Who Is Siva? Understanding God as He

Is Worshipped at Kauai's Hindu Temple," *Hinduism Today,* Dec. 31, 1998, 7.

19. David J. Goa and Harold G. Coward, "Hinduism," *The 1998 Canadian & World Encyclopedia* (Toronto: McClelland & Stewart, 1998).

20. Deborah Kovach Caldwell, "Hinduism the next generation: Born in the U.S.A. Indian Gen-Xers are forcing their faith to come of age," *The Dallas Morning News,* Feb. 20, 1999, 1G.

21. Ibid.

22. "Mr. Eickelman [Dartmouth anthropologist] cites the Syrian Muslim thinker Mohammed Shahrur, who proposes the unifying idea that all believing humans are Muslims in their hearts. 'As long as you don't reject the idea of a Supreme Being, then you are Muslim,' Mr. Shahrur teaches." Larry Witham, "Major changes foreseen in religious expression: Space; The Spirit: Space travel, technology may help to shape," *The Washington Times,* Dec. 31, 1999, A1.

23. Or Sura 5:51 depending on the translation.

24. Norman L. Geisler and Abdul Saleeb, *Answering Islam: The Crescent in Light of the Cross,* 2nd ed. (Grand Rapids, MI: Baker Books, 2002), Logos e-book, 212.

25. There is no doubt that Christ's enemies understood that Christ was calling himself God. On several occasions, as recorded in the gospels (i.e. John 10:36), Christ is accused of blasphemy. If Christ was indeed just a prophet of Allah, or just a great religious teacher, then he would have gone out of his way to make sure that everyone did not misunderstand him when he said he was the "Son of God."

26. Or Sura 5:75 depending on the translation.

27. Or Sura 5:9 depending on the translation.

28. There is no credible historical evidence that the truths in the Holy Bible were tampered with by Christians and Jews as many Muslims believe.

29. Dr. Robert Morey has researched Islam's historical roots and concluded that "Allah" or "Al-ilah" was the name of the moon god, one of more than three hundred gods being worshipped when Mohammed entered Mecca. It is thought that Mohammed threw out all the other gods and proclaimed "Allah" the moon god as the only sovereign god. This is evidenced by the crescent moon on the flags of Muslim countries. Robert Morey, *The Moon-god Allah in the Archeology of the Middle East* (Eugene, OR: Harvest House, 1992), 8, cited by John MacArthur, *Terrorism, Jihad, and the Bible* (Nashville: W Publishing Group, 2001), 41.

IS GOD OBSOLETE?

CHAPTER 5
HAS GOD BECOME OBSOLETE?

1. Barna and Gallup, "It all adds up."
2. Thomas Altizer paraphrased by Patricia Rice and Victor Volland, "Full houses: attendance booms at area places of worship, defying predictions of decline in religion," *St. Louis Post-Dispatch,* Nov. 26, 1995, 01D.
3. In a Gallup poll conducted Jan. 1970, 75 percent of Americans surveyed said religion was losing influence in America. In Feb. 1962, only 32 percent thought the same. "Poll topics and trends: Religion," (www.gallup.com).
4. Rice and Volland, "Full houses."
5. Mary Rourke, "Redefining Religion in America, Part One," *Los Angeles Times,* June 21, 1998, A-1.
6. Geoffrey Parrinder, *The Faiths of Mankind* (New York: Thomas Y. Crowell, 1965), back book flap, orig. pub. under *The World's Living Religions* (Great Britain: n.p, n.d.).
7. Eugene Taylor, "Desperately seeking spirituality," *Psychology Today,* 27 (November 1, 1994), 54–64.
8. Austin, "Easter's Perennial Message."
9. Peter Jennings, "Poll on Importance of Religion in America," *World News Tonight with Peter Jennings,* ABC, March 28, 1997.
10. Katherine Kersten, "More religious than ever? Modern American faith increasingly drained of content," *Minneapolis Star Tribune,* November 20, 1996, 17A.
11. Austin, "Easter's Perennial Message."
12. Barna and Gallup Jr., "It all adds up."
13. Rourke, "Redefining Religion in America."
14. According to Phyllis Tickle, contributing editor in religion at *Publisher's Weekly,* guest on Neal Conan, "Analysis: Post-September 11th spirituality," *Talk of the Nation,* NPR, November 22, 2001.
15. George Gallup Jr., "Religion and Values: Americans Feel Need to Believe," (January 15, 2002), www. gallup.com.
16. "Poll Analyses: Religion in the Aftermath of September 11: A question-and-answer session with George Gallup Jr. and Frank Newport," (December 21, 2001), www.gallup.com.
17. David W. Moore, "'Passion' Viewers Passionate About the Movie: Three in four Americans have seen or expect to see it," *The Gallup Poll Tuesday Briefing* (March 12, 2004).
18. Phil Kloer, "Touched by 'The Passion': As Easter nears, many say Jesus film has changed their lives," *The Atlanta Journal and Constitution,* April 9, 2004, H1.

19. "'Passion of the Christ' Prompts Confession," United Press International, (March 25, 2004).

20. Rick Holland, Question asked of Grace to You. http://www.gty.org/IssuesandAnswers/archive/thepassion.htm (accessed April 11, 2004).

21. Hanna Rosin, "Personal Spirituality," *The Tampa Tribune* (January 29, 2000), 4.

22. George H. Gallup Jr., "Americans' Spiritual Searches Turn Inward," (February 11, 2003), www.gallup.com.

23. D. Michael Lindsay, "Youth on the Edge: A Profile of American Teens (Results of a Gallup Youth Survey)," *The Christian Century, 120* (October 4, 2003), 26.

24. Barna and Gallup, "It all adds up."

25. Cathy Lynn Grossman, "Charting unchurched America," *USA Today,* March 7, 2002, 01D.

26. Ibid.

27. Nolan Zavoral, "Seeking the now: It might look simple, but Zen can be very demanding. In the quiet of meditation, followers attempt to let their thoughts do their own thinking," *Minneapolis Star Tribune,* May 24, 1997, 05B.

28. Ruth Shalit, quoting Showtime's program entitled "Rude Awakening" while she was a guest on National Public Radio (NPR): Ray Suarez, "Angels," Washington, DC, (December 8, 1998). While most of the dialogue from the episode is word-for-word, Ms. Shalit has paraphrased parts of it.

CHAPTER 6
THE GREAT SPIRITUAL
SMORGASBORD

1. D. Martyn Lloyd-Jones, *Love So Amazing* (Lottbridge Drove, England: Kingsway Publications, 1995), 208.

2. Eugene Taylor, "Desperately seeking spirituality," *Psychology Today* 27, (November 1, 1994): 54–64.

3. Richard Cimino and Don Lattin, "Choosing My Religion," *American Demographics* 21 (April 1, 1999).

4. George H. Gallup Jr., "Americans' Spiritual Searches Turn Inward," (February 11, 2003), www.gallup.com.

5. Paul S. Mueller. et al., "Religious Involvement, Spirituality, and Medicine: Implications for Clinical Practice," Mayo Clinic Proc., 2001; 76: 1225–35.

6. Melanie Cooper-Effa, et al., "Role of Spirituality in Patients with Sickle Cell Disease," *J Am Board Fam Pract* 14 (2001): 116–22. A study cited in this article on the subject is Ellison CW., "Spiritual well-being: conceptualization and measurement," *J Psychol Theol II* 11 (1983): 330–40.

7. John MacArthur, "God: Is He? Who is He?" tape # GC 1351, Grace to You.

8. Mary Otto, "A Church away from Church: Home Altars Provide the Intimate Touch for Prayer," *The Washington Post,* January 4, 2004, A1.

9. Cimino and Lattin, "Choosing My Religion."

10. Frank McCourt, "God in America: When You Think of God What Do You See?" *Life,* December 1, 1998, 60.

11. Joseph Carroll, "Religion is 'Very Important' to 6 in 10 Americans," *The Gallup Poll Tuesday Briefing,* June 24, 2004.

12. Michelle Bearden, "Americans Lack Faith in Religion, Poll Shows," *The Tampa Tribune,* January 9, 2003, 1.

13. Albert L. Winseman, "Faith Renewed? Confidence in Religion Rises," *The Gallup Poll Tuesday Briefing,* June 22, 2004.

14. Lloyd-Jones, *Love So Amazing,* 208.

15. Francis A. Schaeffer, *The God Who Is There* (London: Hodder and Stoughton, 1968), 144.

16. Rourke, "Redefining Religion in America."

17. Rosin, "Personal Spirituality."

18. Ibid.

19. Cimino and Lattin, "Choosing My Religion."

20. Paul Johnson, *The Quest for God* (New York: Harper Perennial, 1996), 4, orig. pub. (Great Britain: Weidenfeld & Nicolson, Orion House, 1996).

21. McCourt, "God in America."

22. Kersten, "More religious than ever?"

23. Associated Press, "Most Think God Is the Same in All Religions: Beliefs: A majority in a US survey also say that there is no such thing as absolute truth," *Los Angeles Times,* September 7, 1991, F-15.

24. One source attributes the idea, "God helps those who help themselves" to Benjamin Franklin, while another says it's a proverb in all languages; the earliest use in English was in Algernon Sidney's *Discourse Concerning Government,* 1698. Regardless of who is responsible for the quote, the Bible strongly contradicts it in several passages.

25. Kersten, "More religious than ever?"

26. Carol Eisenberg, "America gets religion (but do Americans get religion?) God talk is everywhere. For some, it's a spiritual awakening; for others, a pop-culture commodity," *Newsday,* April 12, 2004, B02.

27. Barna and Gallup, "It all adds up."

28. Jon Tevlin, "New Age, new market: The boom in so-called New Age or alternative spirituality has spurred a soaring consumer market that includes everything from angel books to aura adjustments," *Minneapolis Star Tribune,* October 24, 1999, 01E.

29. "Year of Spirituality 2003–2004 (Presbyterian Church of Canada

launches program of spirituality)," *Presbyterian Record,* July 1, 2003.

30. Tevlin, "New Age, new market."

31. Cimino and Don, "Choosing My Religion."

32. Eisenberg, "America gets religion."

33. Stephen Batchelor summarized in Jeff Dawson, "Devout's not out anymore: Hollywood gets religion," *The Dallas Morning News,* April 11, 1998, 3C.

34. Gaouette, "Japan's Search for Spirituality."

35. United Press International. "Religious Service Attendance Dropping," January 15, 2000.

36. *Herald Sun,* (Melbourne, Australia) "Old-time religion loses its appeal for Aussies," June 19, 2000, 025.

37. Julie Ray, "Worlds Apart: Religion in Canada, Britain, U.S.," *The Gallup Poll Tuesday Briefing,* August 12, 2003.

38. Peter Ford, "Churches on wane in Europe," *The Christian Science Monitor,* October 25, 1999, 1.

39. 1999 Gallup survey cited in Josephine Mazzuca, "Worship Call: Do U.S., Canada, and Britain Answer?" (October 15, 2002), www.gallup.com.

40. Ford, "Churches on wane in Europe."

41. Phil Zuckerman, "Secularization: Europe—yes, United States—no. Why has Secularization occurred in Western Europe but not in the United States? An examination of the theories and research," *The Skeptical Inquirer* 28 (March 1, 2004): 49–52.

42. Ford, "Churches on wane in Europe."

43. "Religious Service Attendance Dropping," United Press International, January 15, 2000.

44. Philip Jenkins, "The changing face of Christianity: Faith's center of gravity is shifting from the West to the South and East," *The Dallas Morning News,* April 8, 2000, 1G.

45. Sinikka Kahl, "A Place to Feel at Home: Africa's Independent Churches," *The World & I* 10 (December 1, 1995): 194.

46. Hank Hanegraaff, *Counterfeit Revival* (Dallas: Word, 1997), 9–10.

47. "In Asia, shocking new charismatic cults are springing up, blending Buddhism, Taoism, Confucianism, and other teachings with Western Charismatism. The charismatic movement as a whole is entirely unequipped to defend against such influences. For in the charismatic movement, unity is a question of shared religious experience, not doctrine. If doctrine doesn't matter, then why not embrace Buddhist Charismatics?" John MacArthur, "Does God Promise Health and Wealth?" Part II (Grace to You, 1991), tape # GC 90–64.

CHAPTER 7
THE BIG PICTURE

1. "Letters," *Life,* February 1, 1999, 12.
2. Arthur W. Pink, *Gleanings in the Godhead* (Chicago: Moody Press, 1975), 28.
3. Ibid., 13.
4. Andrew M. Greeley, *Confessions of a Parish Priest* (New York: Simon and Schuster, 1986), 435–36.
5. Michael Shevack and Jack Bemporad, *Stupid Ways, Smart Ways to Think About God* (Liguori, MO: Triumph Books, 1993), 53.
6. David Heller, *Talking to Your Child About God* (New York: Bantam Books, 1988), 68.
7. David Heller, *Dear God: Children's Letters to God* (New York: Berkley Publishing Group), 24, orig. pub. (New York: Doubleday, 1987).
8. Richard Dawkins paraphrased in Paul Johnson, *The Quest for God* (New York: Harper Perennial, 1996), 94; orig. pub. (Great Britain: Weidenfeld & Nicolson, Orion House, 1996).
9. Ibid., 61.
10. Martha Fay quoted in Allison Adato and Miriam Bensimhon, "Features/Life Special: Kids' Pictures to God," *Life,* March 1, 1998, 68.
11. Karen Armstrong, *A History of God: The 4000-Year Quest of Judaism, Christianity and Islam* (New York: Alfred A. Knopf, 1994), 356.
12. 2003 Ipsos-Reid poll quoted in Gabrielle Bauer, "God & Other Mysteries," *Reader's Digest* (Canada), November 2003, 50–59.
13. Adato and Miriam, "Kid's Pictures to God."
14. Shevack and Bemporad, *Stupid Ways, Smart Ways to Think About God,* 9.
15. Kersten, "More religious than ever?"
16. Paul Greenberg, "Diagnosis by the therapeutic society," *The Washington Times,* August 31, 1998, A15.
17. Douglas Todd writes, "Now, in the thick of a religion-fueled war with Muslims on one side and Christians and Jews on the other, some secular people are saying it's time to slam the brakes on religion, and maybe get rid of it outright." In Douglas Todd, "Put your faith in faith: Some are blaming religion for much of the world's woes, but science verifies that spirituality is good for you beyond what it can do for your soul," *Vancouver Sun,* October 10, 2001, A15.
18. Gaouette, "Japan's Search for Spirituality."
19. "Year of Spirituality 2003–2004."
20. Sohail Inayatullah quoted in Larry Witham, "Major changes foreseen in religious expression: Space; The Spirit: Space travel, technology may help to

shape," *The Washington Times,*
December 31, 1999, A1.

CHAPTER 8
SOLOMON'S CLUES

1. Kathleen Norris, "Lessons from
next-year country," *U.S. News
& World Report* 123 (December
15, 1997): 70.

Additional copies of *Is God Obsolete?*
and other Victor titles
are available wherever good books are sold.

❧

If you have enjoyed this book,
or if it has had an impact on your life,
we would like to hear from you.

Please contact us at:

VICTOR BOOKS
Cook Communications Ministries, Dept. 201
4050 Lee Vance View
Colorado Springs, CO 80918

Or visit our Web site:
www.cookministries.com

Victor®
The Bible Teacher's Teacher